The Beauty of New Zealand's South Island

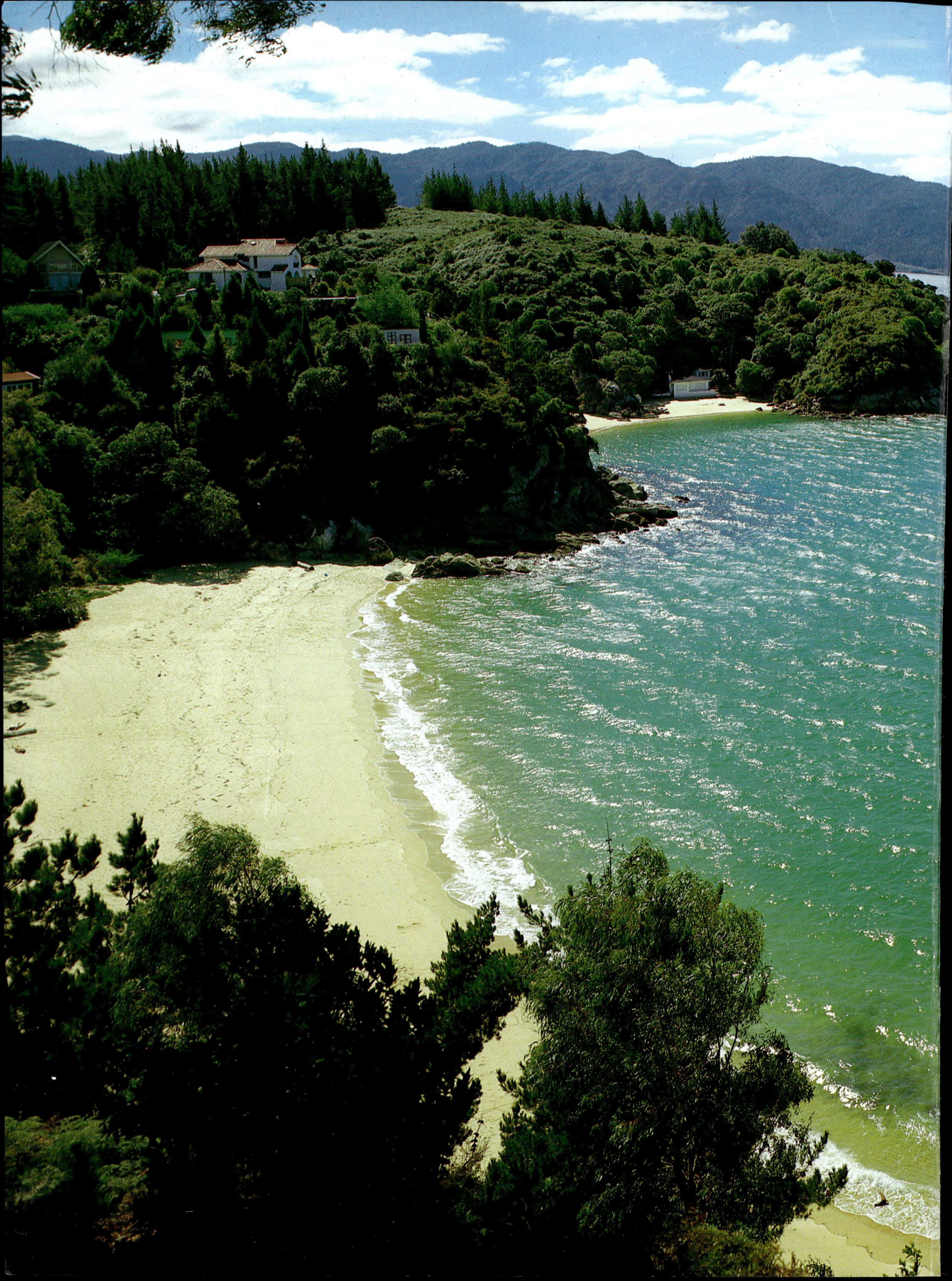

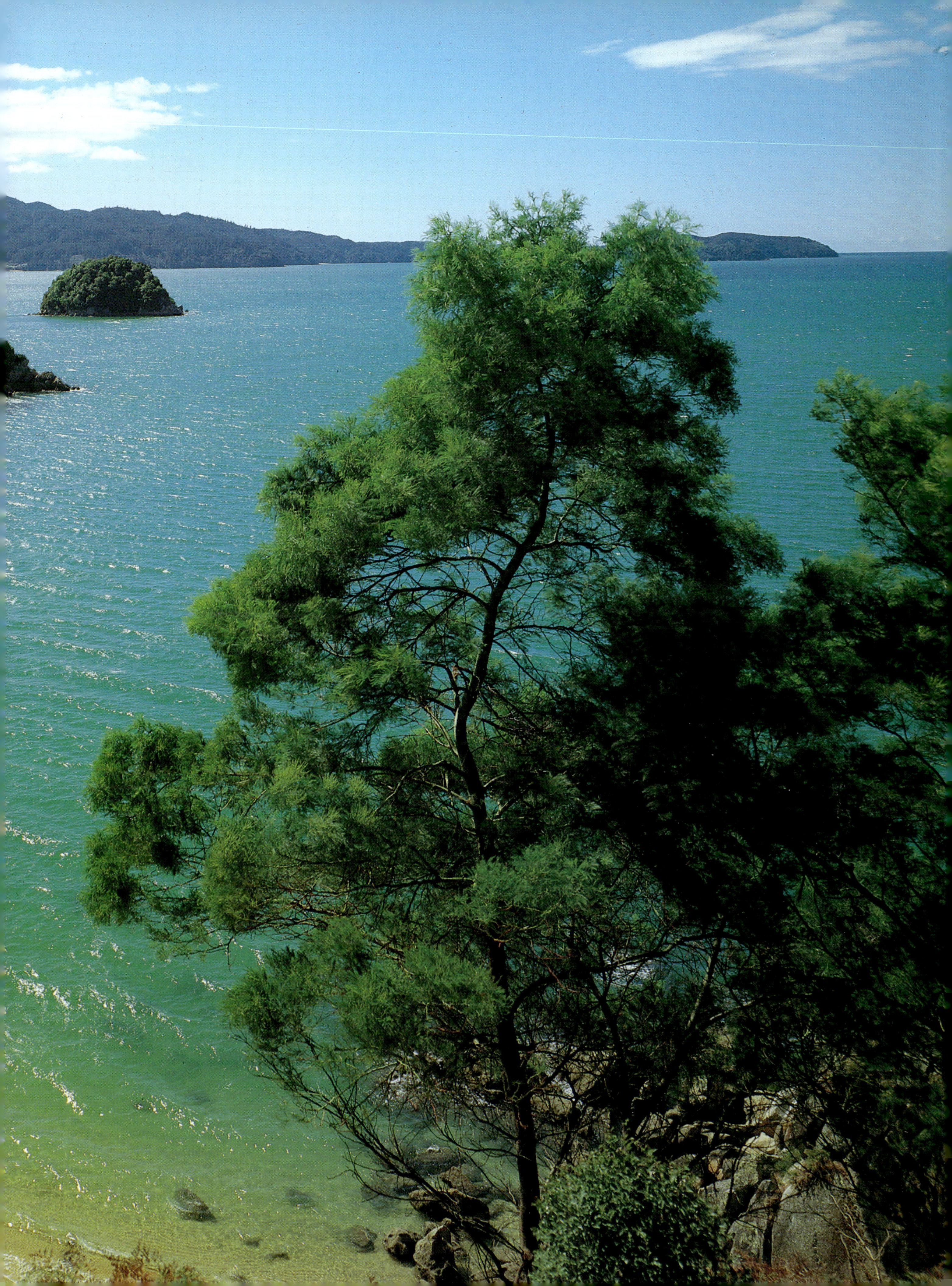

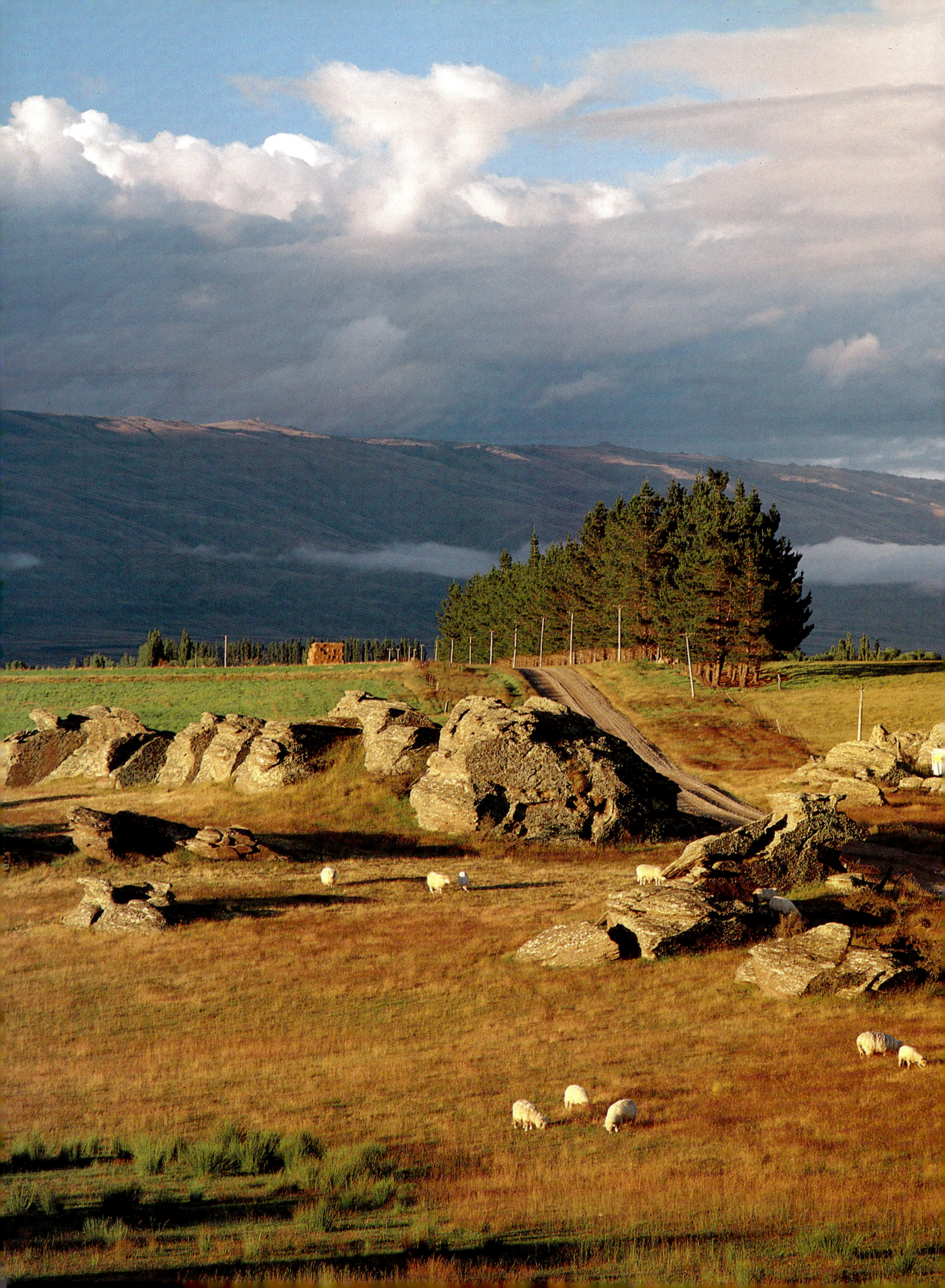

The Beauty of New Zealand's South Island

Warren Jacobs
text by
Errol Brathwaite

KOWHAI

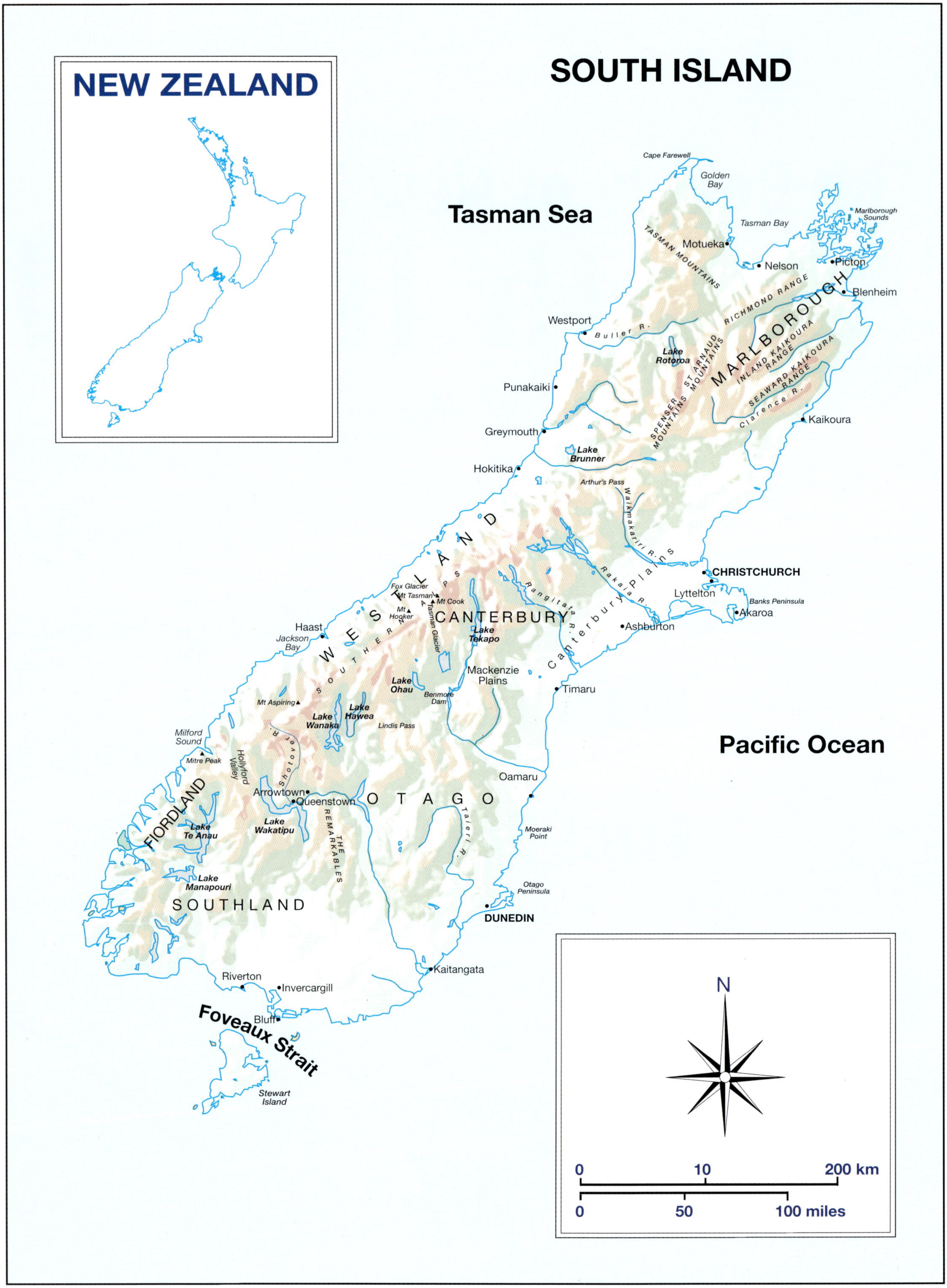

NEW ZEALAND
SOUTH ISLAND
Tasman Sea
Pacific Ocean
Cape Farewell
Golden Bay
Tasman Bay
Marlborough Sounds
Motueka
Nelson
Picton
Blenheim
TASMAN MOUNTAINS
RICHMOND RANGE
MARLBOROUGH
INLAND KAIKOURA RANGE
SEAWARD KAIKOURA RANGE
Clarence R.
Kaikoura
ST ARNAUD MOUNTAINS
SPENSER MOUNTAINS
Westport
Buller R.
Lake Rotoroa
Punakaiki
Greymouth
Lake Brunner
Hokitika
Arthur's Pass
Waimakariri R.
CHRISTCHURCH
Lyttelton
Banks Peninsula
Akaroa
Rakaia R.
Canterbury Plains
Ashburton
Rangitata R.
WESTLAND
SOUTHERN ALPS
Fox Glacier
Mt Tasman
Mt Cook
Mt Hooker
Tasman Glacier
CANTERBURY
Lake Tekapo
Haast
Jackson Bay
Mackenzie Plains
Lake Ohau
Benmore Dam
Timaru
Mt Aspiring
Lake Wanaka
Lake Hawea
Lindis Pass
Milford Sound
Mitre Peak
Hollyford Valley
Shotover R.
Oamaru
Arrowtown
Queenstown
OTAGO
Taieri R.
THE REMARKABLES
FIORDLAND
Lake Te Anau
Lake Wakatipu
Moeraki Point
Lake Manapouri
SOUTHLAND
Otago Peninsula
DUNEDIN
Kaitangata
Riverton
Invercargill
Bluff
Foveaux Strait
Stewart Island
N
0
10
200 km
0
50
100 miles

Contents

Front cover: Lake Alexandrina
Back cover: Southern Alps
Pages 2–3: Kaiteriteri Coast
Page 4: Rock and Pillar Range near Sutton, Otago

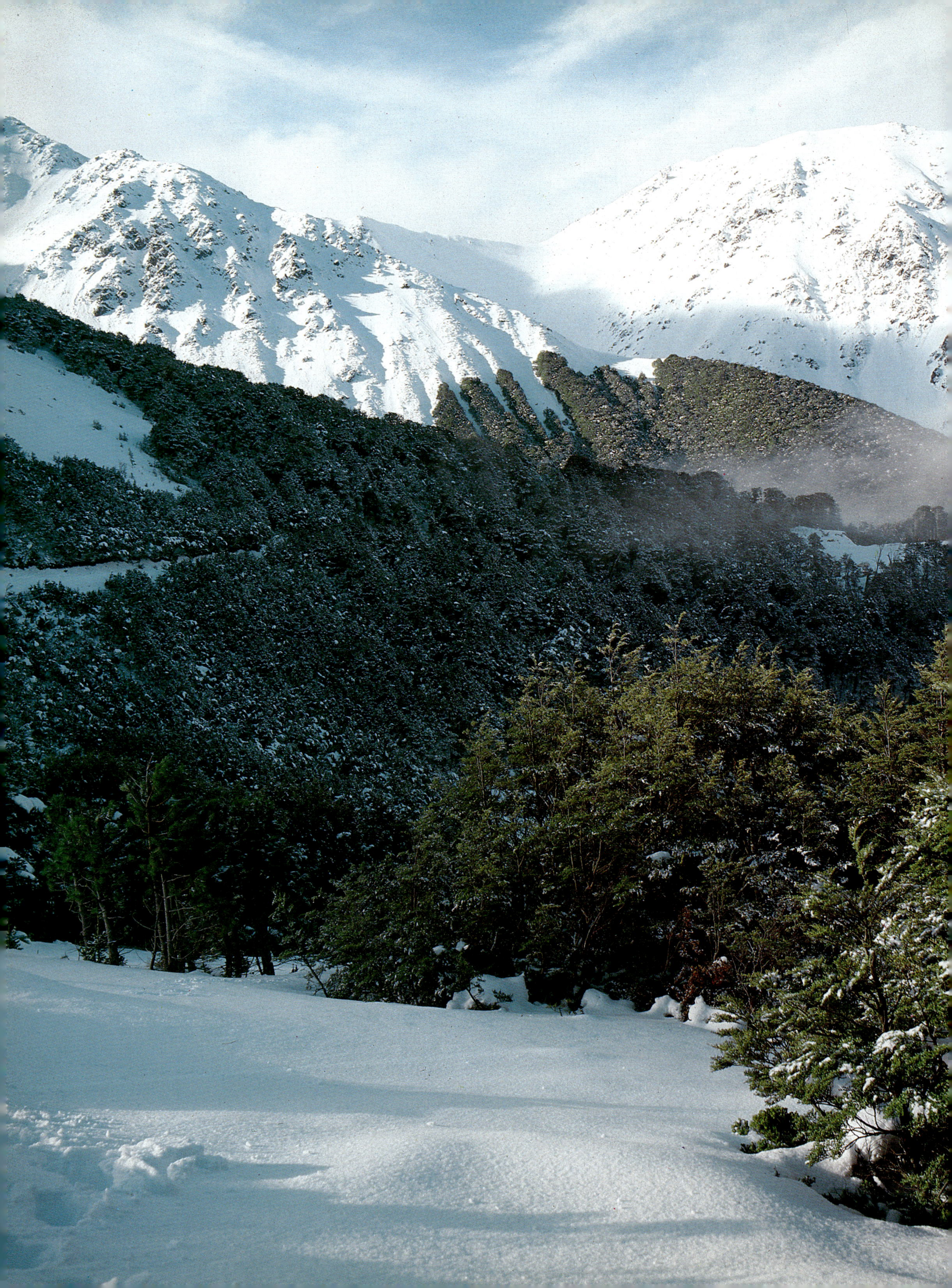

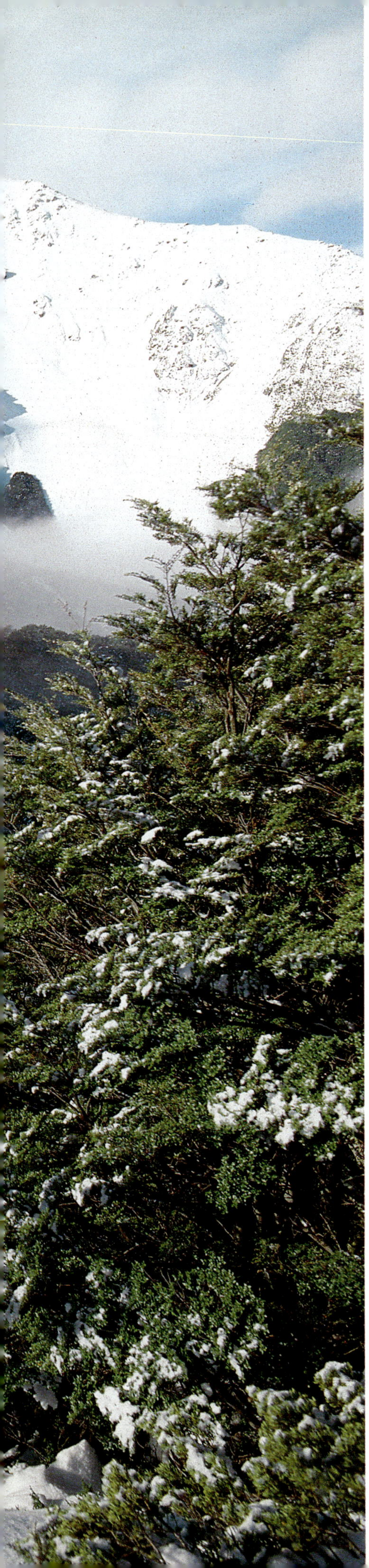

A Perfection of Grandeur

FIRST-TIME visitors to New Zealand, describing their impressions, might well say, simply, 'The country is mountainous.' It wouldn't be telling the full tale, but such a description would convey a fairly adequate picture. New Zealand is mountainous; and even in those areas where it is not, its plains, coastlines, lakes, cities and rolling pastoral landscapes are brooded over, dominated by mountains. Where the eye looks inland, it is usually guided on and upwards to a high, serrated skyline, sometimes dark with forest to the crests of notched ridges, sometimes dazzling with year-round snow. Single summits, or prides of powerful peaks, mountains are the predominant feature, the key component which establishes the character of the entire scene.

This, in varying degrees, is true of both North and South Islands. But it is in the South Island that the mountains reach a perfection of grandeur. The South Island is more spectacularly creased than the North Island. Viewed from almost any internal airline flight, vast areas of the South Island are seen to be as crumpled as a discarded piece of paper, with range upon range of titanic pressure-fold ridges stretching away as far as the eye can see. The Tasman Mountains, the Richmond Range, the St Arnaud and Spenser Mountains and the Kaikoura Ranges fan out northward from the great rugged chain which forms the Southern Alps. At their southern end the Alps fray out into a wild and well-nigh impenetrable tangle of mountains covering perhaps half of the Otago-Southland region.

The Southern Alps, of course, take pride of place. They are the show-piece, the magnificent spectacle, that attracts visitors in their awed thousands. In their folds they hold lakes of unrivalled splendour. On their valley-riven flanks, between their massive lateral arms, they cradle splendid glaciers. In this massif alone there are more than 130 peaks that rise over 2400 metres (7872ft), chief of which is Aoraki, the Cloud-Piercer, officially and prosaically named Aoraki/Mt Cook (after the great eighteenth-century navigator) by official and prosaic Captain Stokes of the survey ship *Acheron*, in the mid-nineteenth century.

It is the mountains, of course, that order the country's climate. The South Island is exactly what its name describes, a southern ocean island, with an island's capricious weather patterns. That is to be expected. What is astonishing, however, is the number of climatic variations, distinct climatic zones, within such a small compass; for the island is a mere 750km (465 miles) long by 250km (155 miles) wide at its widest point. And that – by continental terms – is a small area in which

LEFT: SNOWFALL, CRAIGIEBURN RANGE, CANTERBURY

The Craigieburn Range, high above Lake Lyndon on the road to Arthur's Pass, is a drab area in summer, more like a gigantic gravel heap than an alpine spur. But in winter, when the snow is down into the valleys, it is at once majestic and magical, like everyone's dream of Switzerland.

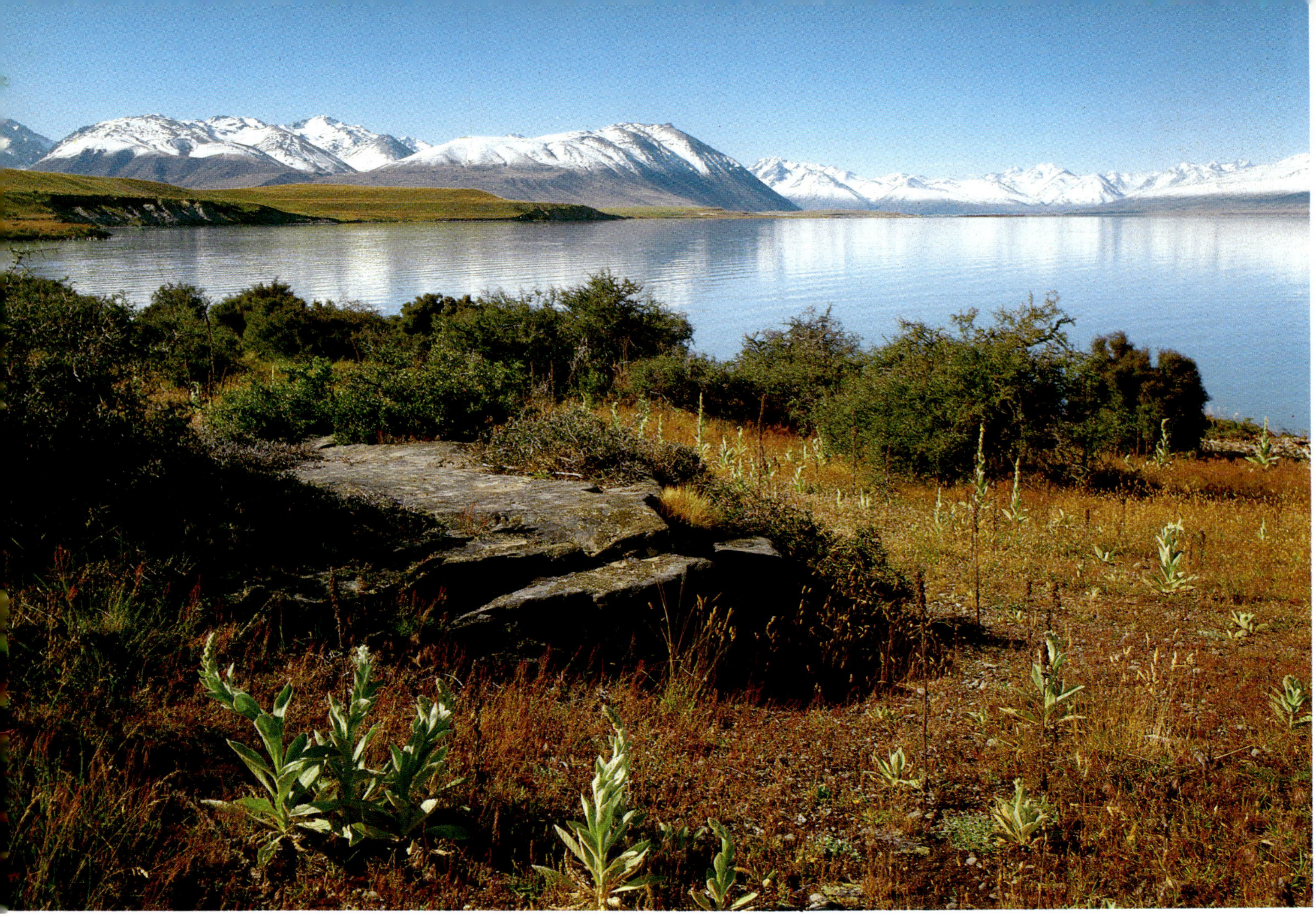

Above: Lake Tekapo, Mackenzie Country

A true alpine lake, Lake Tekapo was once an ancient glacier, a prehistoric ice-burden which the surrounding countryside has never quite forgotten or forgiven. Near the lake edge, feathery snowgrass, foxglove and the spiny matagouri seem to be the only plants willing to inhabit the thin soil covering the ancient moraine.

Right: Glendhu Bay, Lake Wanaka

Though the autumn days are warm, the shingly beach of Glendhu Bay is deserted by evening, when the last rays of the lowering sun are defeated by the early evening chill. The cold comes creeping across the deep waters of Lake Wanaka which, it is suddenly easy to recall, was once a mass of glacier ice, thousands of metres thick.

to have, side-by-side, zones which are: temperature in climate, with a moderate to low rainfall; areas which are dry to the point of being near-desert; areas of immoderately high rainfall and lush forest of almost sub-tropical luxuriance; areas which experience each winter a heavy and sustained snowfall; areas of crackling frosts; and areas with an enviable tally of annual sunshine hours.

The moisture-laden winds from the Tasman Sea bring clouds which are literally trapped on the western side of the Southern Alps, and are forced to such altitudes that they unload heavy rains onto the narrow coastal strip on the mountains' western side. The north-west winds, buffeting their way through mountain valleys as though gigantic wind-tunnels, burst upon the eastern plains with great and sometimes destructive force. The eternal snows upon those prodigious peaks refrigerate the winter air, so that east-coast towns, cities and farmlands receive crisp frosts on clear nights from late March till late September.

No South Islander lives more than two or three hours' drive from ski-slopes, ice-bound skating ponds and lakes and hillsides that are snowy from July to October. Few have not at least a nodding acquaintance with the high country, and some memorable experiences of the great ranges. At the very least, they will have memories of some mountain mood or spectacle, such as the first rays of the morning sun touching Aoraki/Mt Cook's summit with flame while the land is still dark, or the reflected brightness of the moonlight on the snow-clad face of the Remarkables, or the snow-covered peaks of the Kaikouras seeming to lean over the calm bay. No matter where South Islanders live – on the broad, billiard-table-flat plains of Canterbury, the rolling hills of North Otago, the rock-bound Kaikoura coast, the high uplands of the Mackenzie Country, the rock-ribbed, glacier-planed terraces of Central Otago, or in the bustling towns and cities – every South Islander is, in some special way, a child of the mountains.

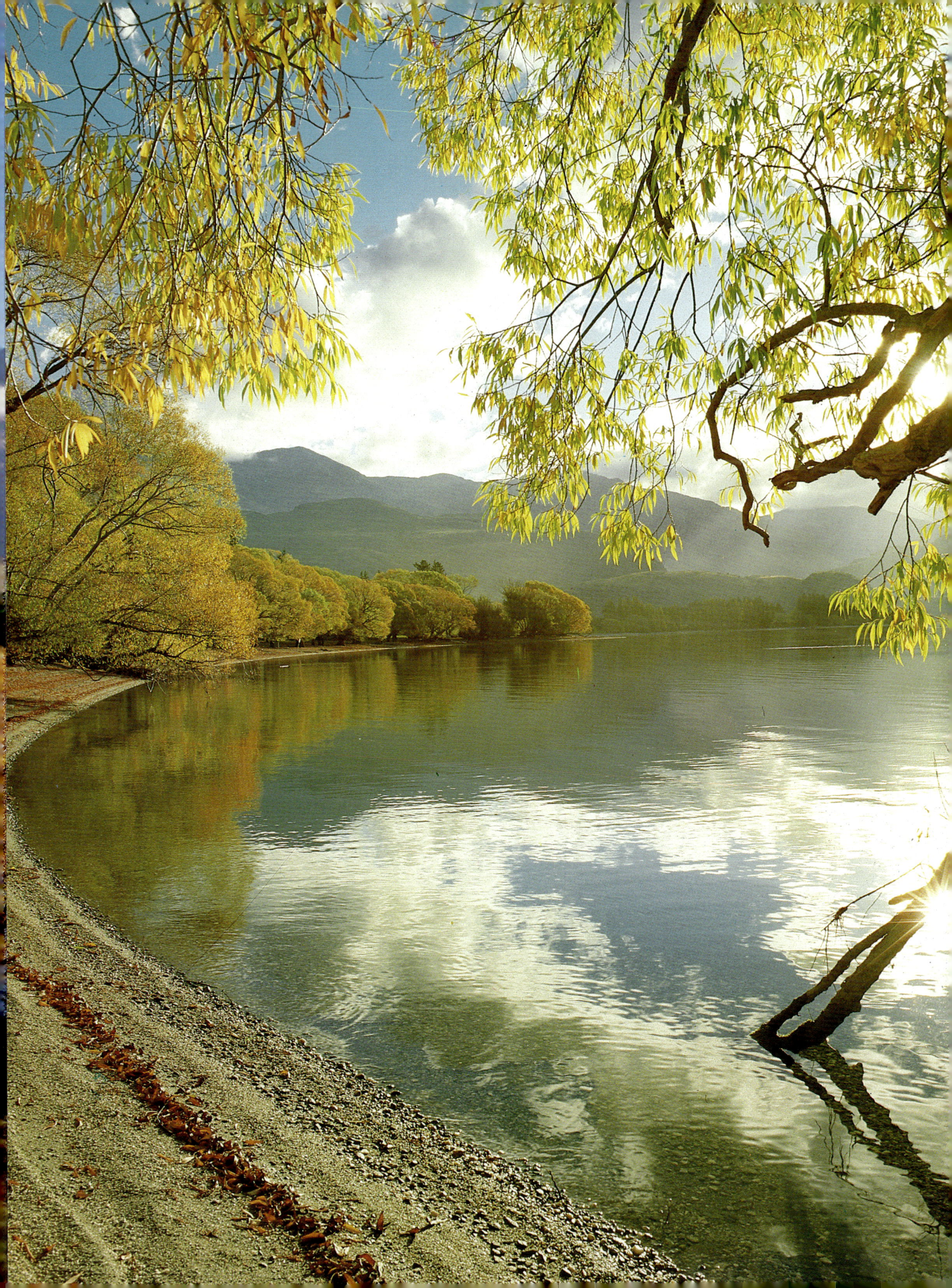

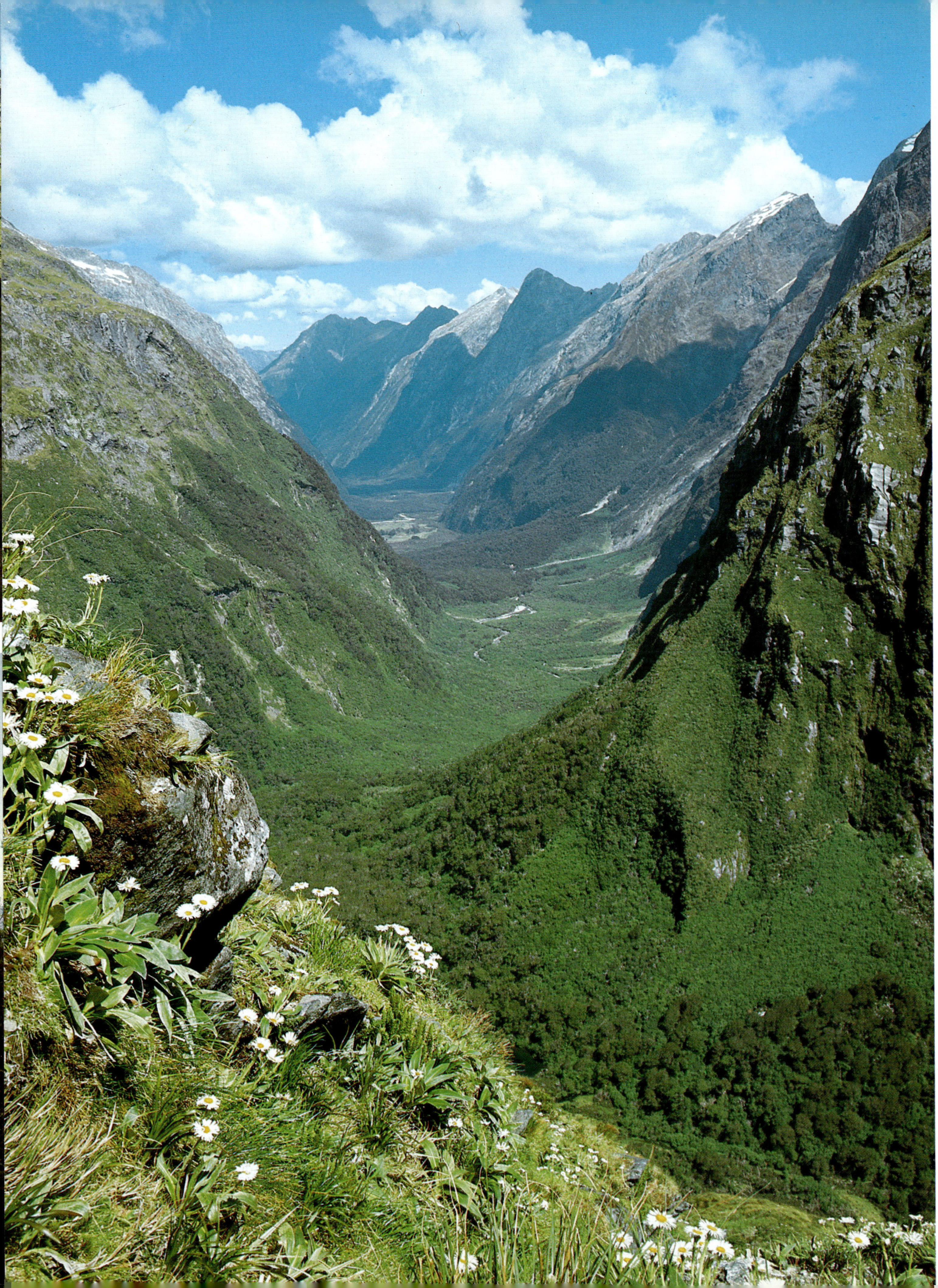

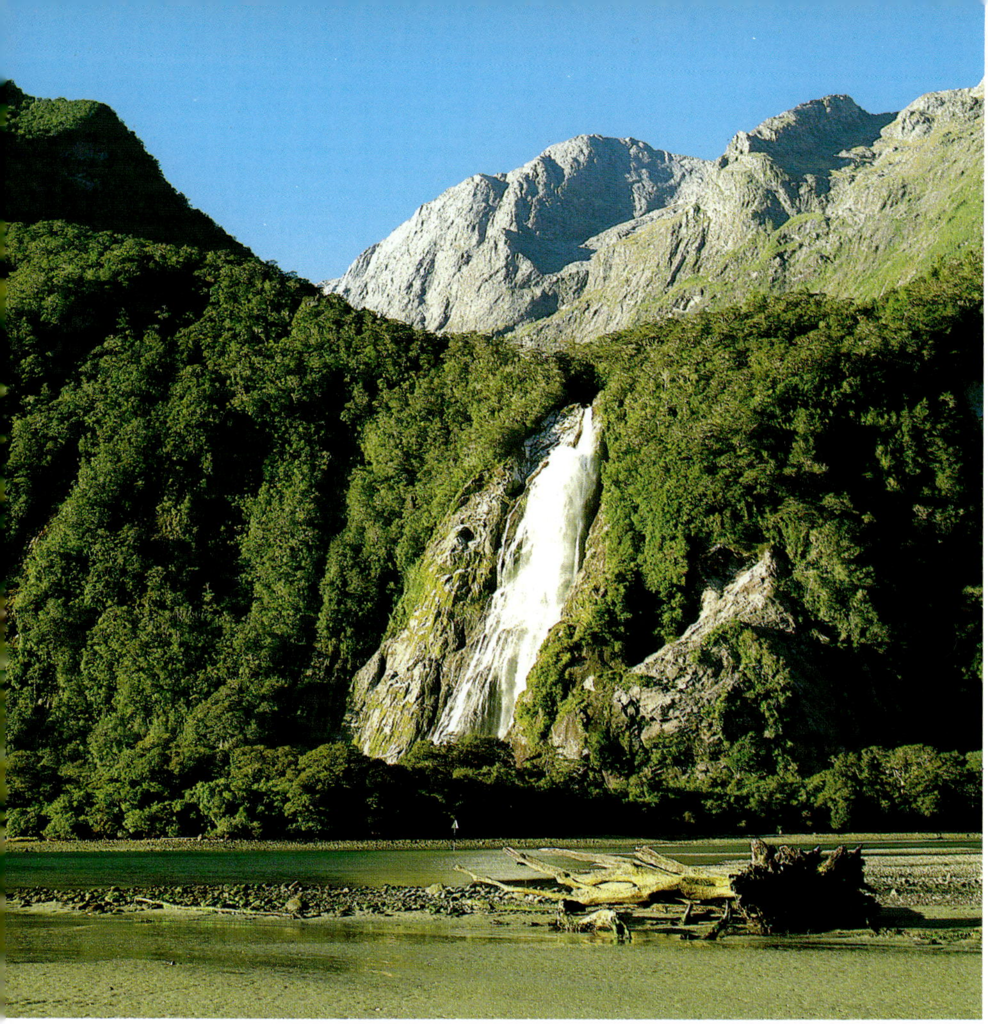

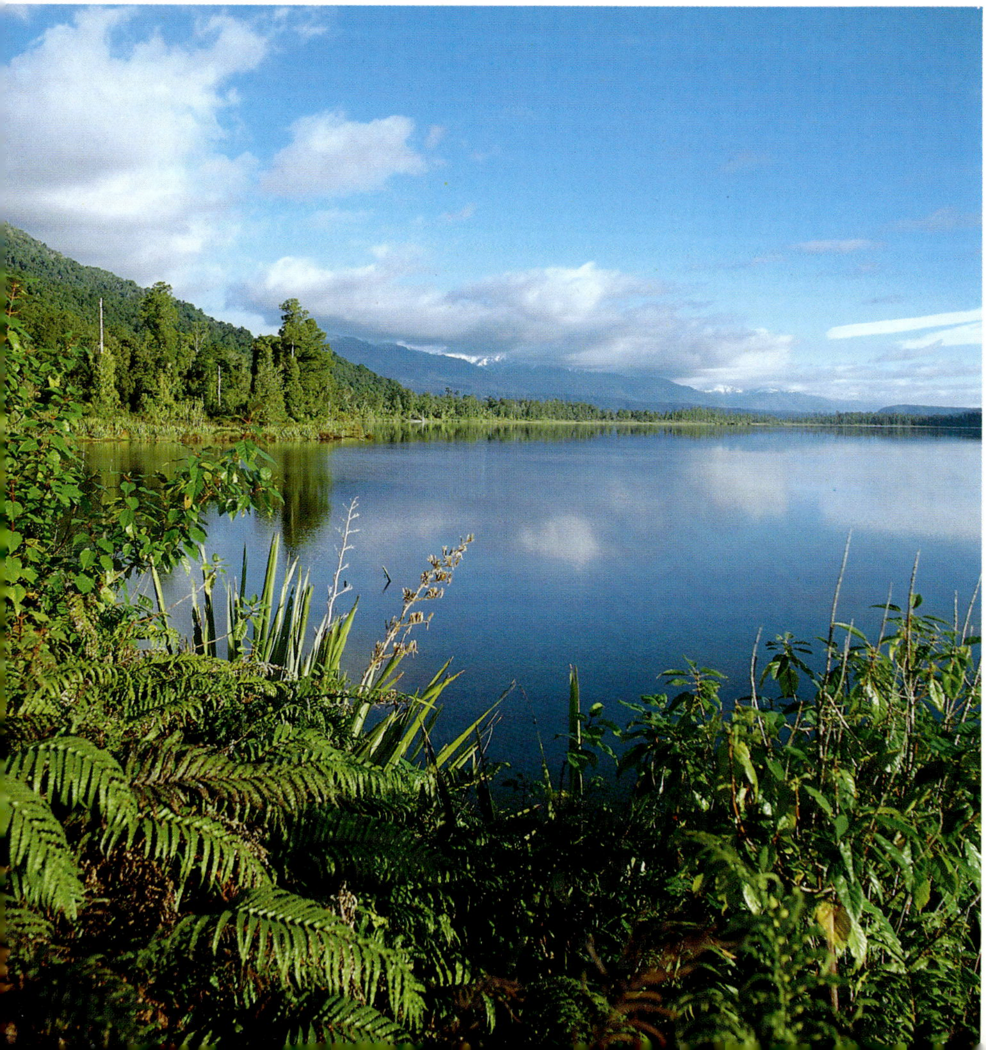

LEFT: BOWEN FALLS, MILFORD SOUNDS

Bowen Falls issue from a hanging valley high above the head of Milford Sound. The water plunges first onto an inclined, hollow rock 'springboard', from which it leaps out again in a sparkling white arc, to fall into a spray-clouded basin. The leap is most dramatic after rain; but even when the water is draped over the rocky faces of the gash in the forested mountain wall, it is hardly less beautiful.

BELOW: LAKE IANTHE, WESTLAND

Set in a scenic reserve about 15km (9 miles) from Harihari, this delightful little gem of a lake was named, it is said, by a surveyor-explorer who admired Byron's 'Childe Harold's Pilgrimage', which was dedicated to a little girl named Ianthe. If that seems to be a roundabout way of arriving at a name, perhaps it was just that the little lake's exquisite smallness (5.6 square km/2 square miles), by its very contrast with the grandeur of the mountains, brought to mind simple and charming things.

FAR LEFT: CLINTON CANYON, MILFORD TRACK

Part of the famous Milford Track winds beside the Clinton River for 23km (14 miles) through the mountain-walled valley known as the Clinton Canyon. The forested mountains rise straight up from the valley floor for perhaps 1200m (3940ft), then lean back as they stab skyward with spear-point peaks to some 1800m (6000ft) above sea level. The canyon climbs, eventually, to Mackinnon Pass, reaching up through moss-hung, twisted mountain beeches to an open area of ranunculus and mountain daisies, where keas come close, unafraid and friendly.

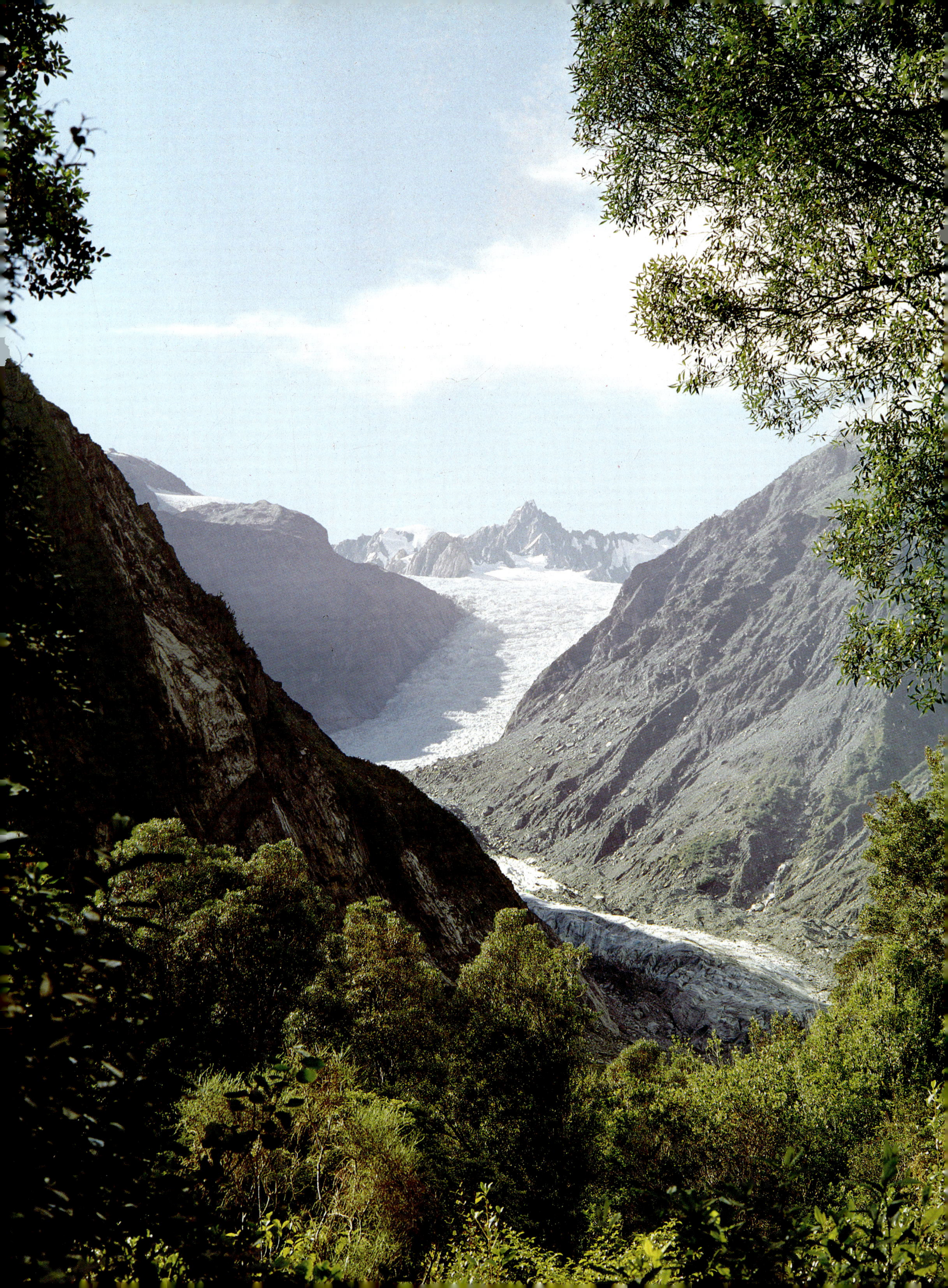

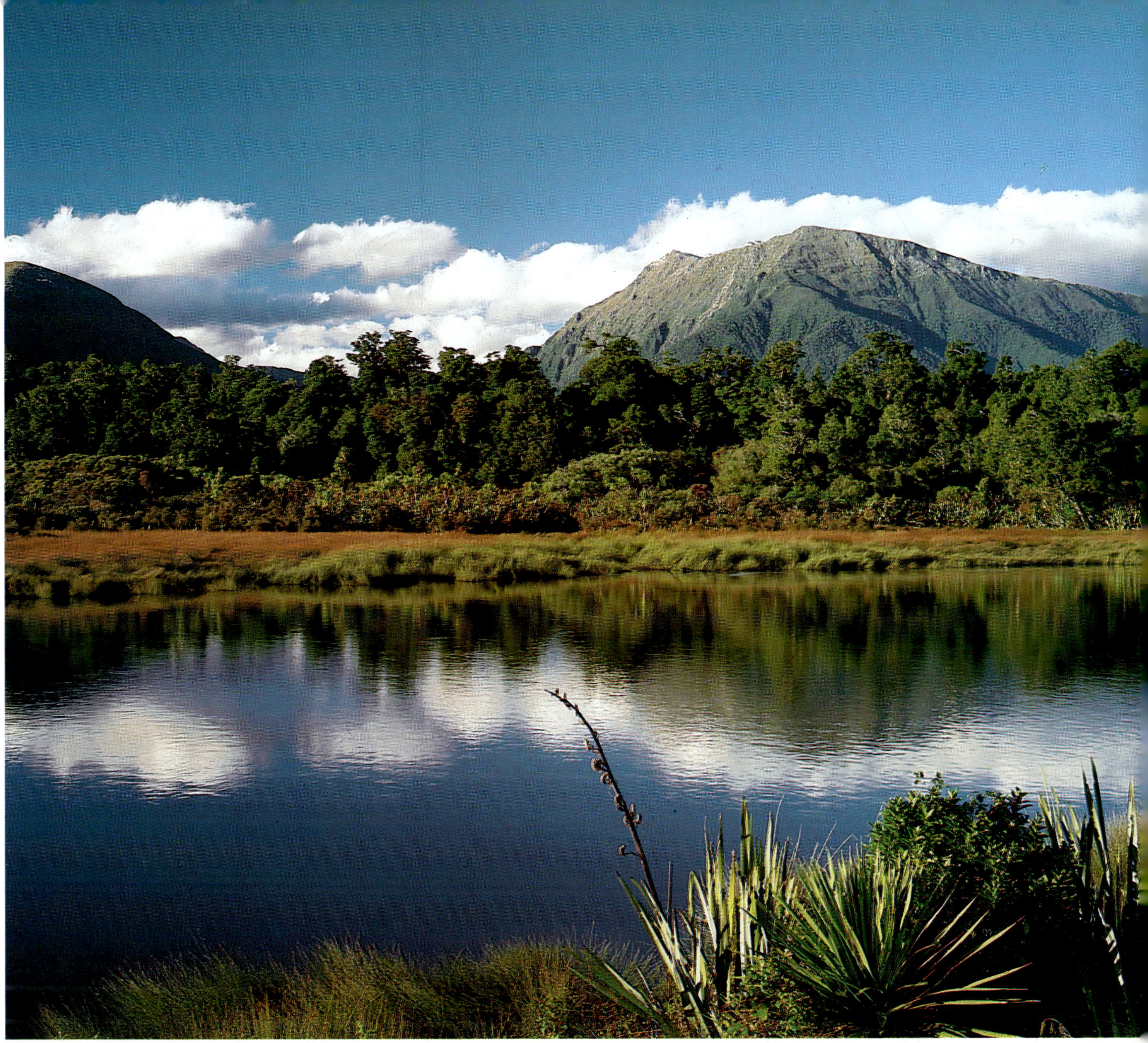

LEFT: FOX GLACIER

Fox Glacier's somewhat zig-zagging course brings the great ice-river down from the neve, the vast snowfields in their inclined basin between the Fritz and Fox Ranges, to a landscape of spurs covered with forest of almost tropical luxuriance. From the glacier's terminal face issues the Fox River, bursting out from an ice cave, carrying great chunks of ice as it hurries down to join the Cook River.

ABOVE: THE OKURU RIVER AND SOUTH WESTLAND MOUNTAINS

From Okuru, south of Haast, the great forested humps of hill stand up above bush and swamp to form outriders of Mt Aspiring National Park, southern extremity of the Alps proper. This is untouched country – the snow-fed river, swelled by many a tributary creek, slides across the coastal flats, flanked by sedges and flax, with a backing of shrubs, which in turn give way to tall forest trees.

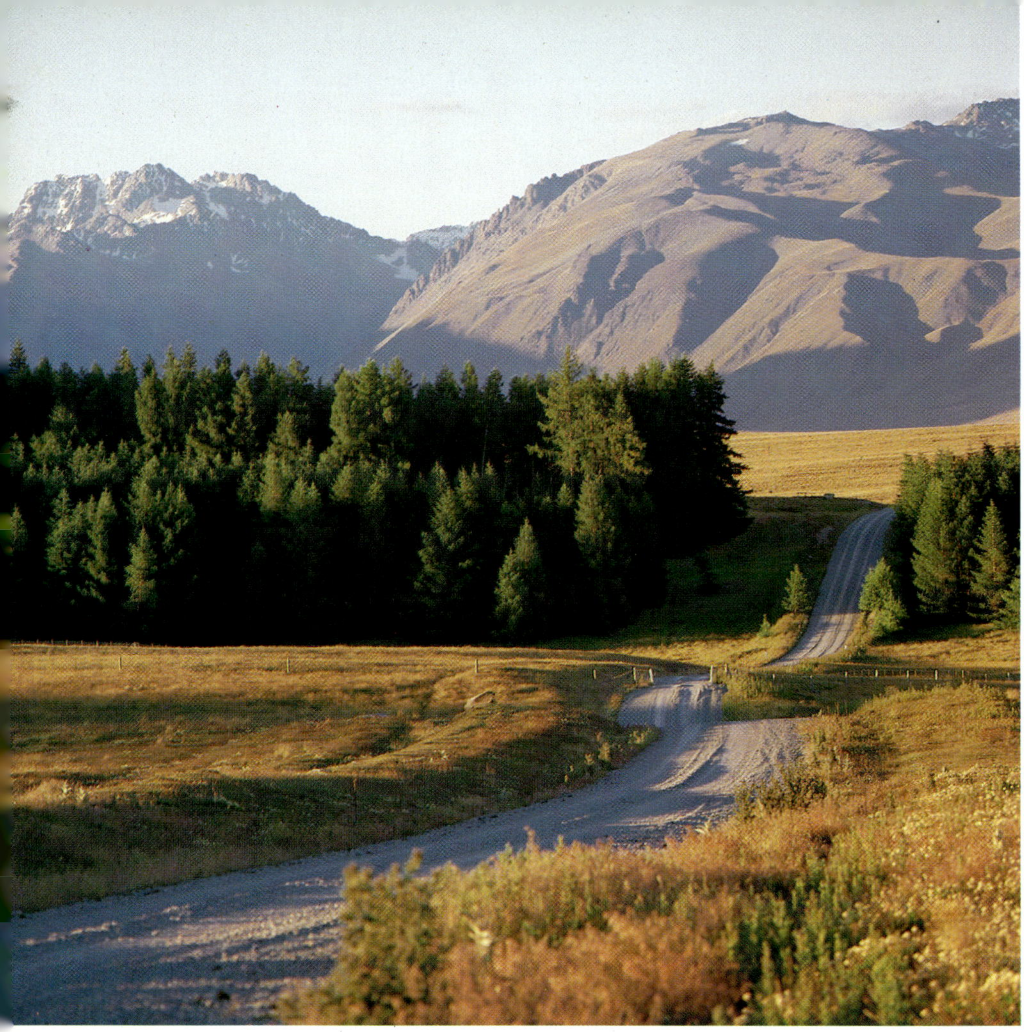

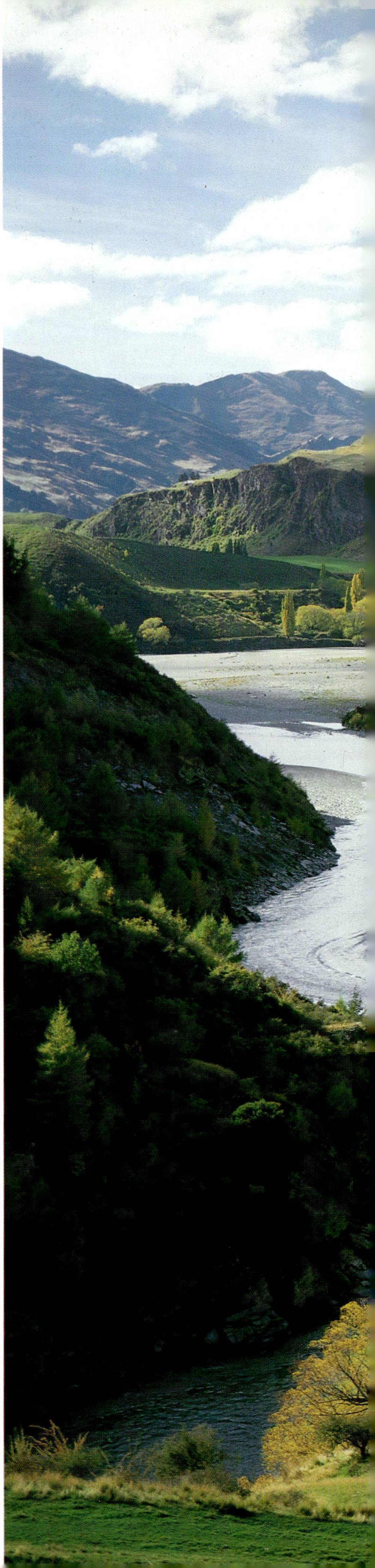

ABOVE: HIGH-COUNTRY ROAD NEAR GLENMORE STATION, MACKENZIE COUNTRY

Towards the head of Lake Tekapo, the Godley Peaks rise up from the Mackenzie Country landscape of brown snowgrass and tussock, and the shelter belts of dark, hardy pines. The peaks are snow-covered in winter, but in summer are eroded and barren, like gigantic heaps of gravel, crumbling slowly to choke the Canterbury rivers and build up the vast gravel flats of the Mackenzie Basin.

RIGHT: SHOTOVER RIVER AT ARTHUR'S POINT, CENTRAL OTAGO

All the fascinating contradictions of the Central Otago landscape show in the Shotover River's writhing valley, near Queenstown. Here are the typical rock-ribbed hills, furred with brown, sun-scorched grasses and patched with matagouri and tough briars. Here are the poplars and willows, autumn-yellow from the first frosts; and amidst the harshness there is, here and there, the lush green of a cultivated field. But always, winding across the scene, are the Central Otago rivers, depositing their frequently gold-bearing gravels at the feet of rocky, broom-clad spurs.

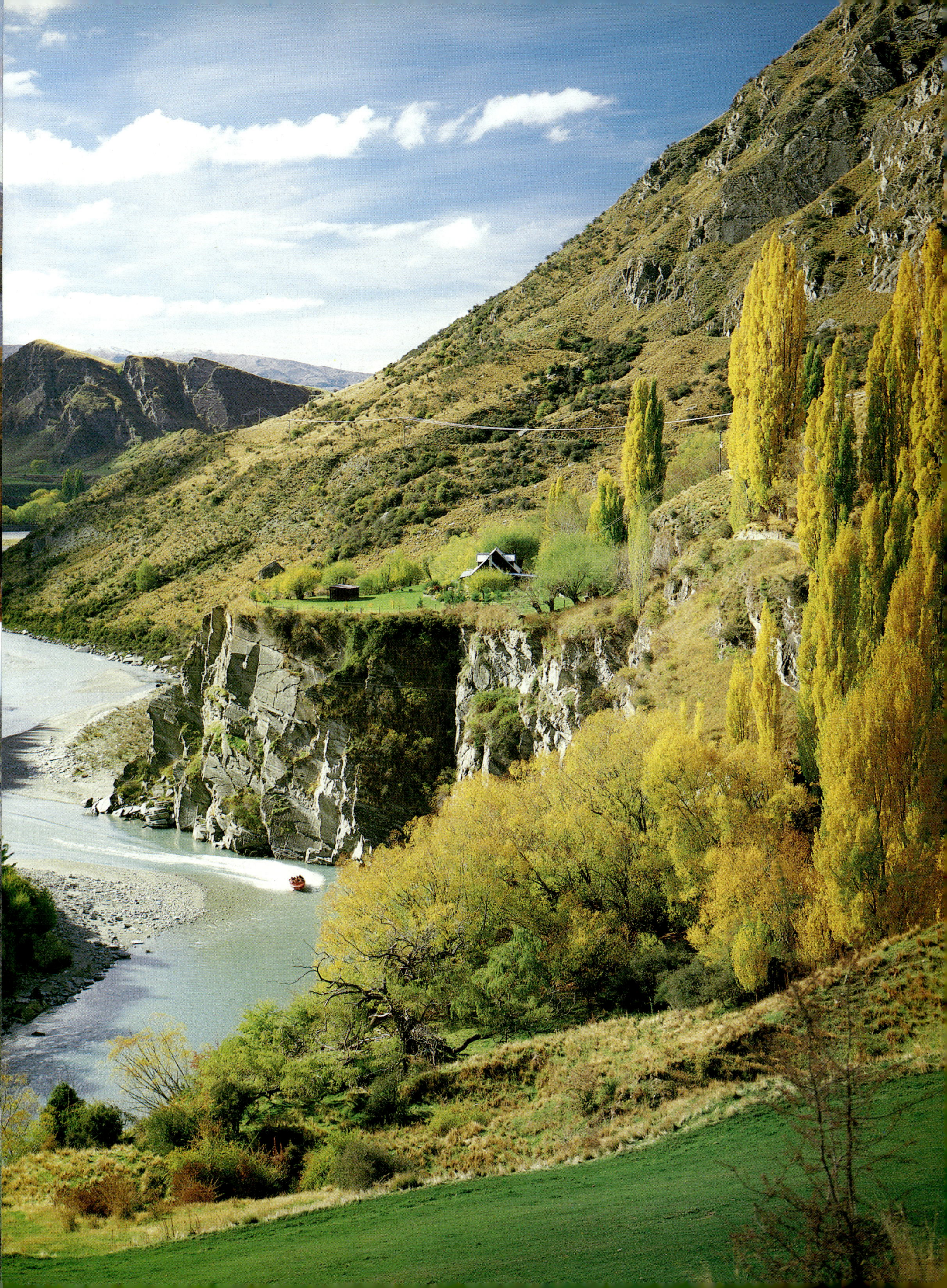

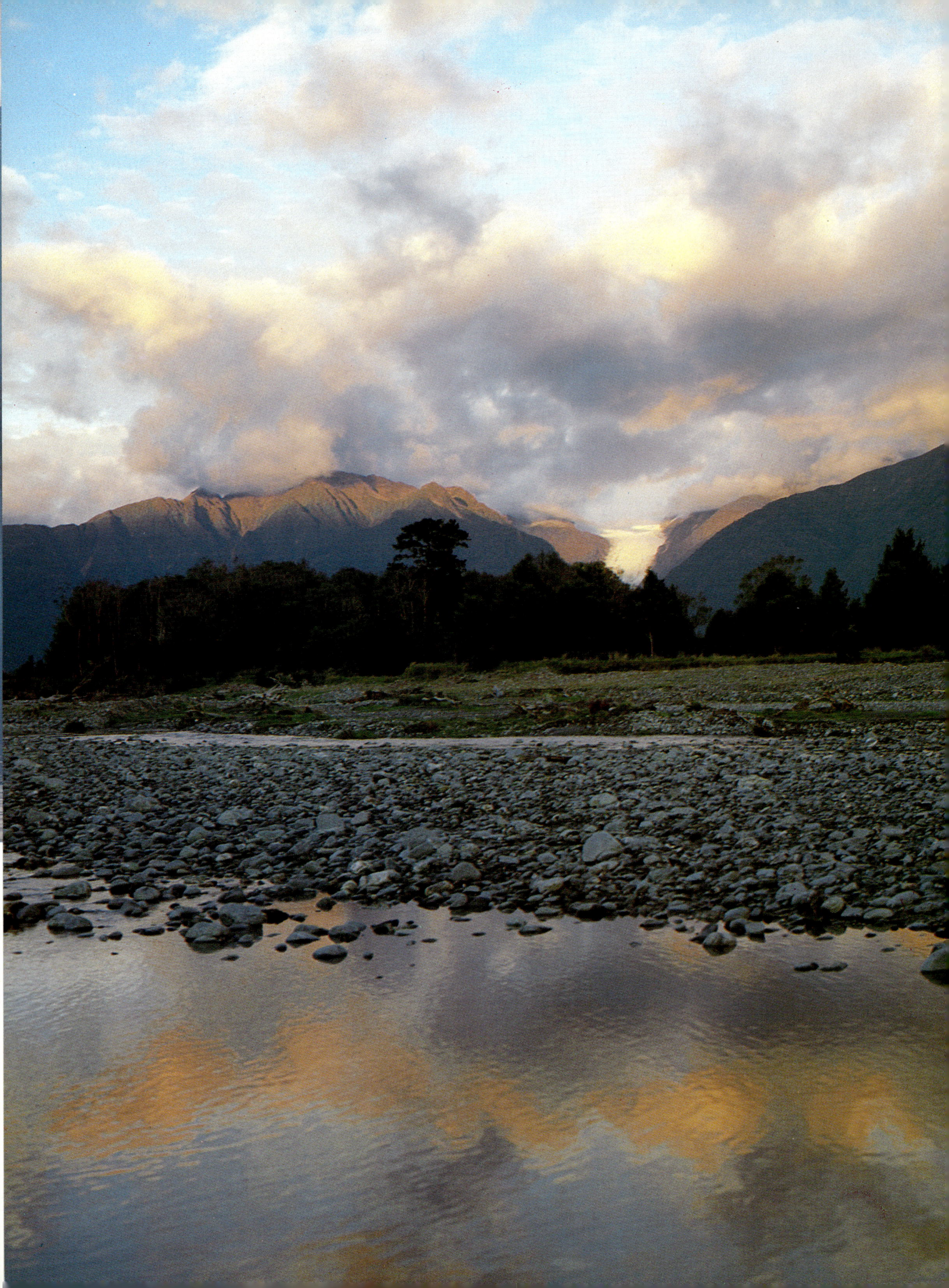

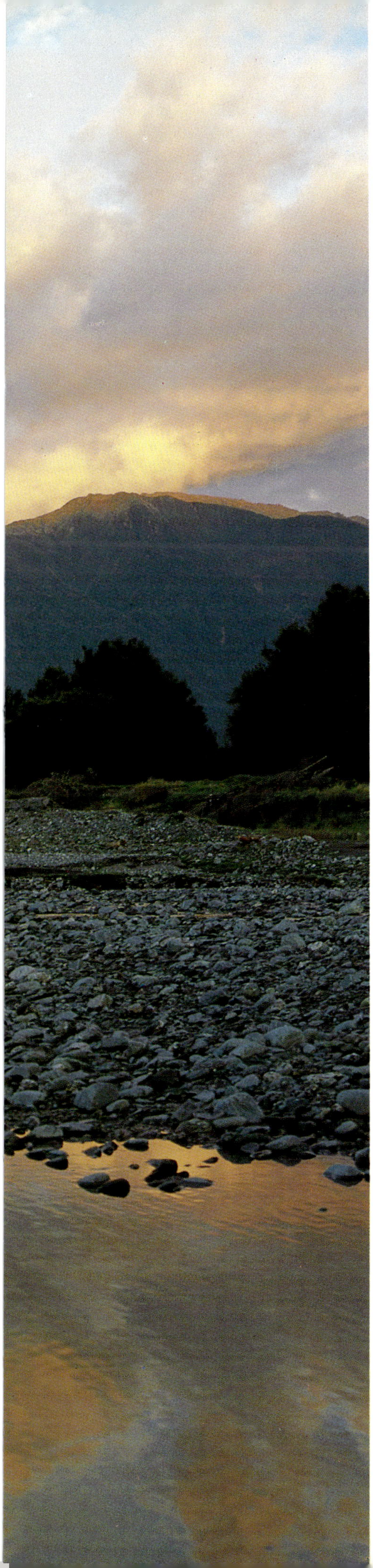

LEFT: FOX GLACIER FROM CLEARWATER FLAT

The Clearwater River rattles over stony shallows along the edge of a typical Westland river flat, which it shares with the Cook River. Its waters reflect the almost theatrical spectacle of clouds slowly parting like stage curtains to reveal, first the Fox Glacier in its notch in the granite mountains, and then the splendour of the stupendous peaks from which the glacier flows.

BELOW: MT TASMAN, FROM FOX, SOUTH WESTLAND

The peaks of the Southern Alps are never more spectacular, never more clearly, magnificently displayed, than they are from South Westland, that narrow coastal shelf at their very feet. Mt Tasman, 3498m (11 475ft), cradles on its faces the snows which feed the Balfour and Abel Janzoon Glaciers, the latter spilling down into the vast neve which gives birth to the mighty Fox Glacier.

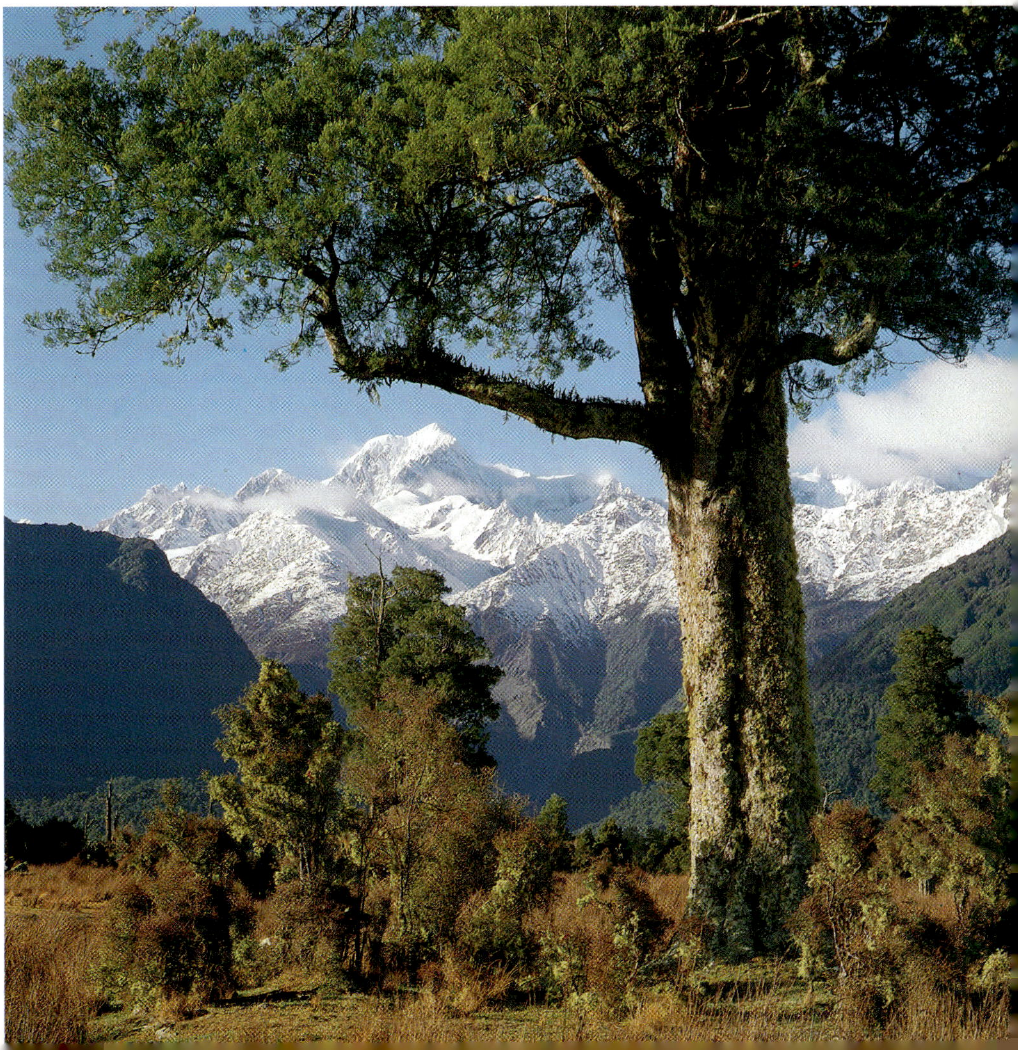

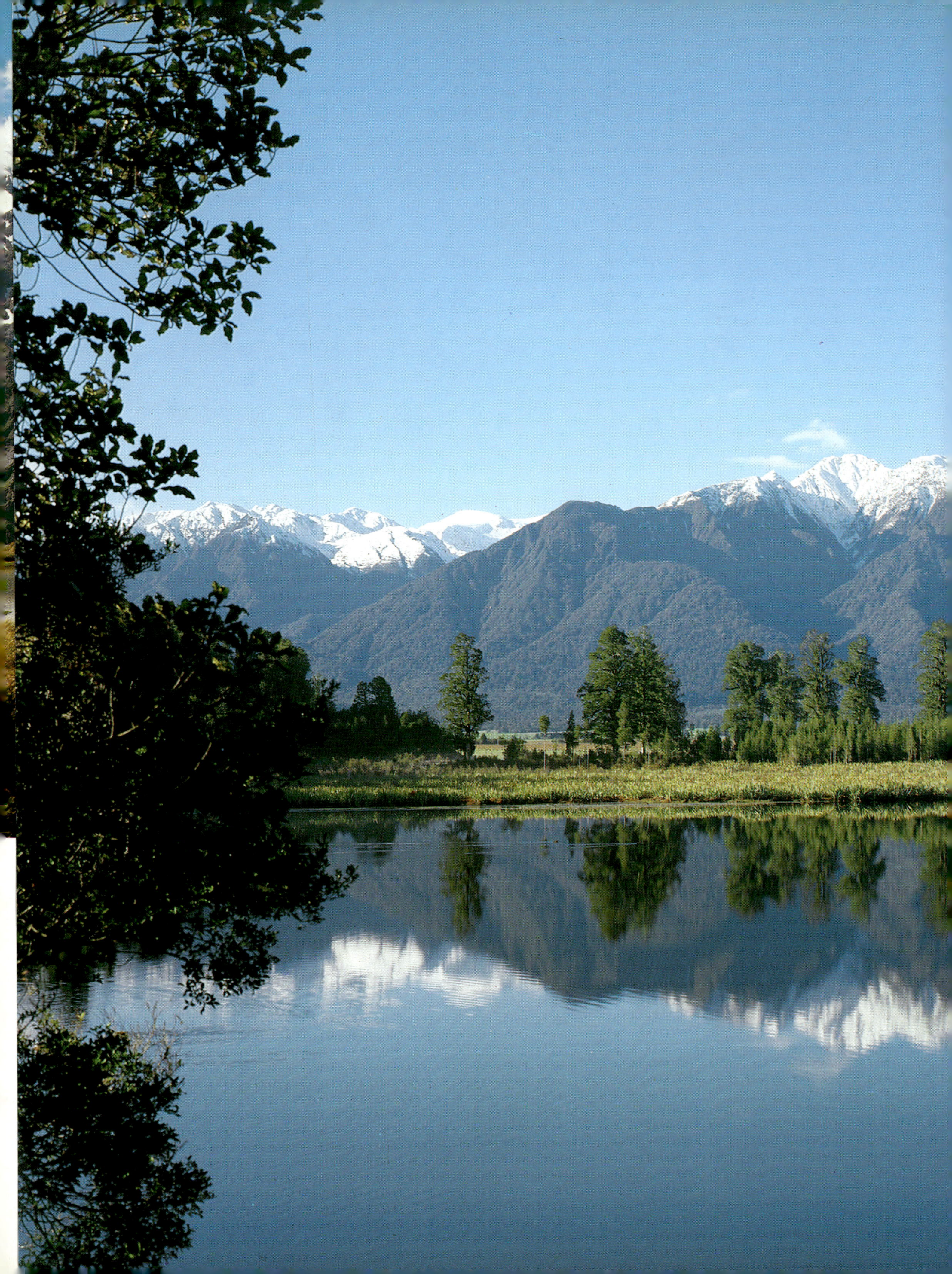

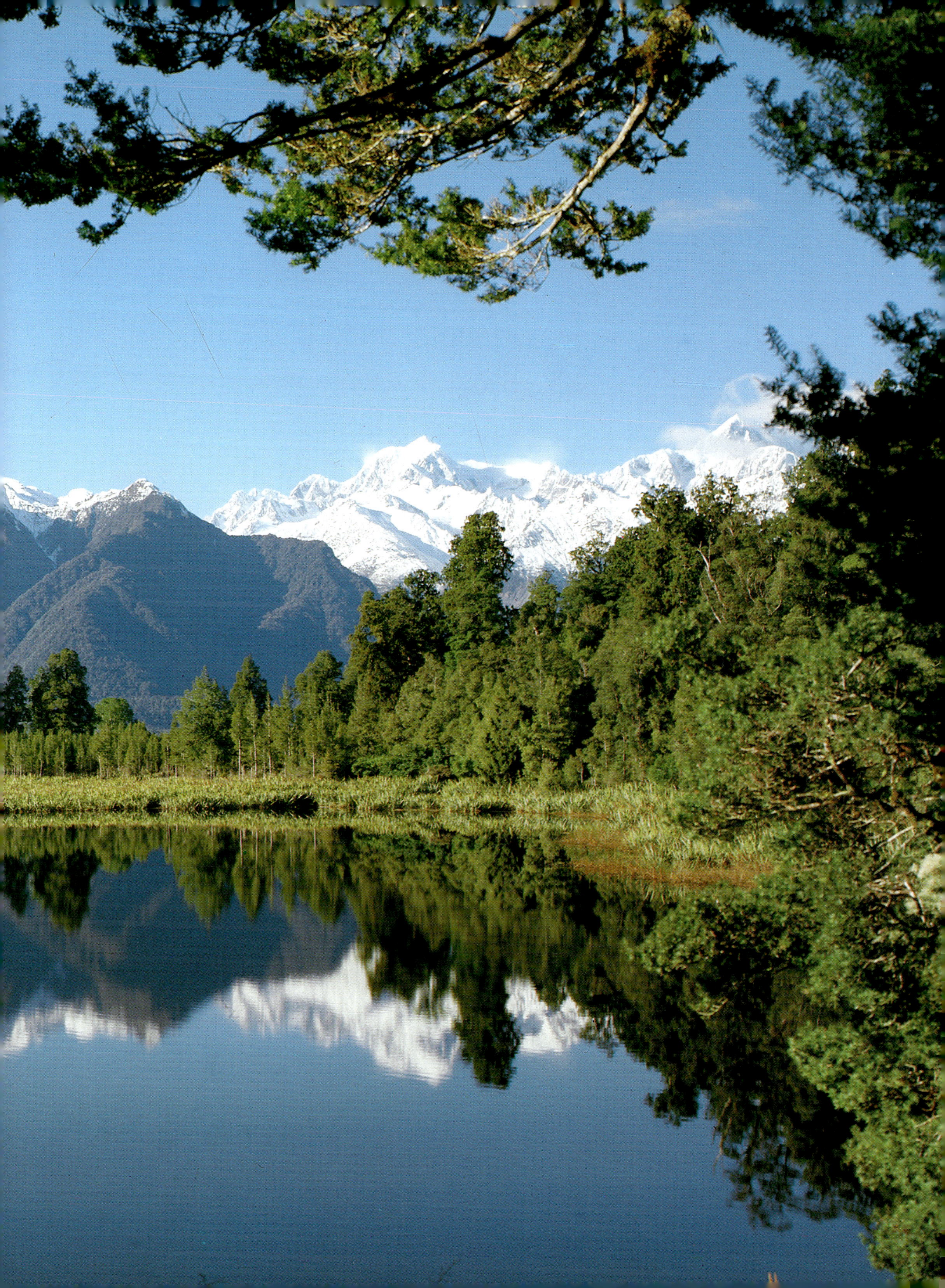

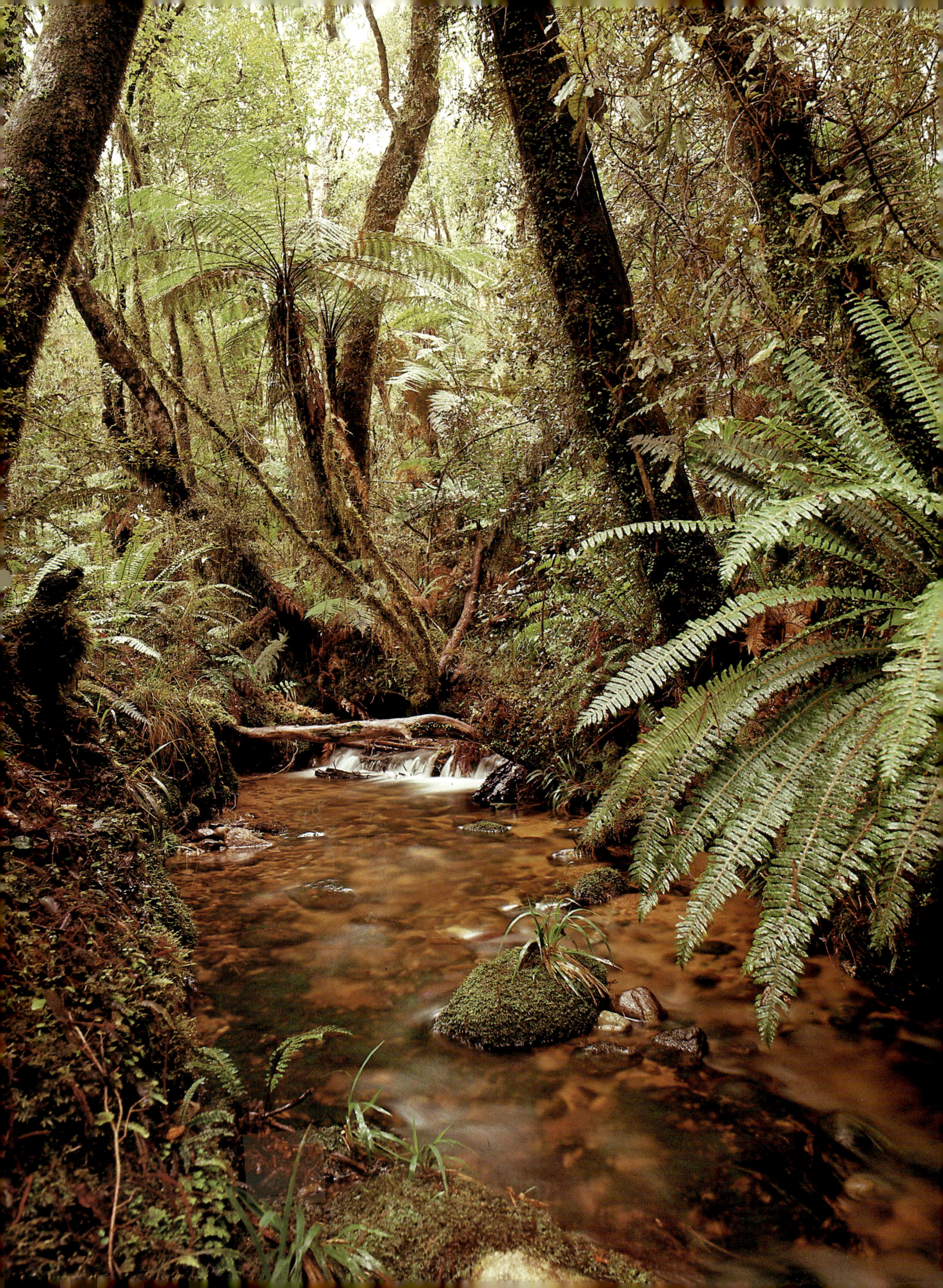

LEFT: WESTLAND BUSH AND STREAM

On the western side of the ranges, where the rainfall is frequent and heavy, the bush has an almost tropical luxuriance. Living trees are coated, furred, festooned with parasitic growth. Dead forest giants lie on the forest floor, crumbling beneath a burden of fungi and mosses. An unbelievable variety of ferns peer from flying-buttress root systems of trees, or reach for the sky on rough, palm-like trunks. Strange and riotous growth clothes mossy banks and droops from host trees; and the whole struggling growth fights upward, competing for a share of sunshine.

BELOW: LAKE BRUNNER FROM LONE TREE LOOKOUT, WESTLAND

When they found it in its high setting of forested foothills, Europeans named it Lake Brunner. The Maori, perhaps more alive to the poetry of its calm beauty, had long before named it Moana Kotuku, the Sea of the White Heron. Whatever it is called, the beautiful water is a vista of calm loveliness. It spreads across 26 square km (10 square miles) and is the largest of all the Westland lakes. It is constantly replenished by the run-off of Westland's heavy and frequent rains in the surrounding mountains.

OVER ABOVE: SHEEP MUSTERING BENEATH AORAKI/MT COOK, MACKENZIE COUNTRY

In the Canterbury high country, Merino sheep graze all through summer on the sparse, sun-ripened grasses, foraging over the tops of hills which, in another country, would be listed among the high mountains. But Aoraki/Mt Cook, snow-covered even in high summer, and the central massif of the Southern Alps gaze down upon the dun-coloured pastures, and their snows chill the breath of the westerly winds.

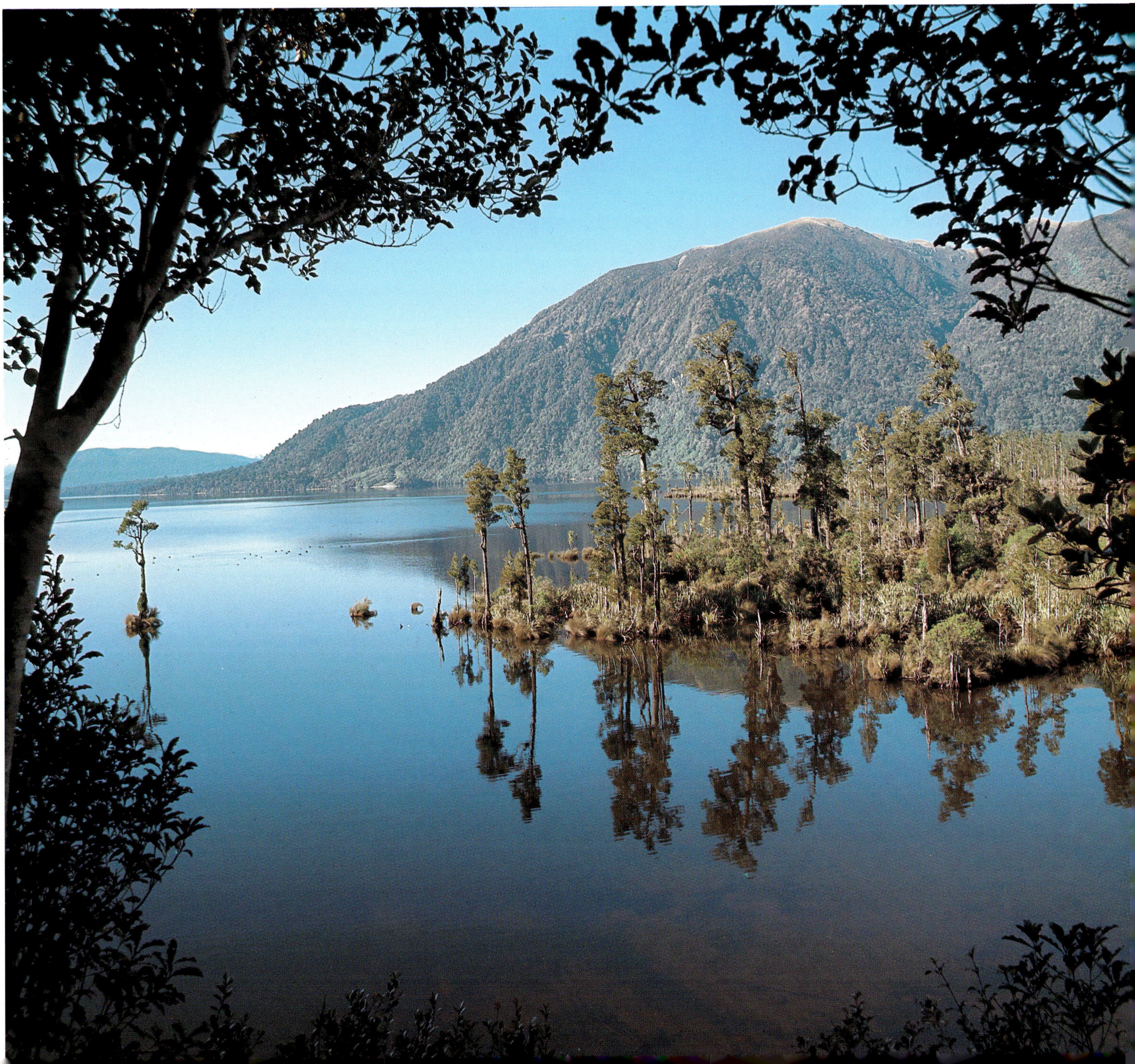

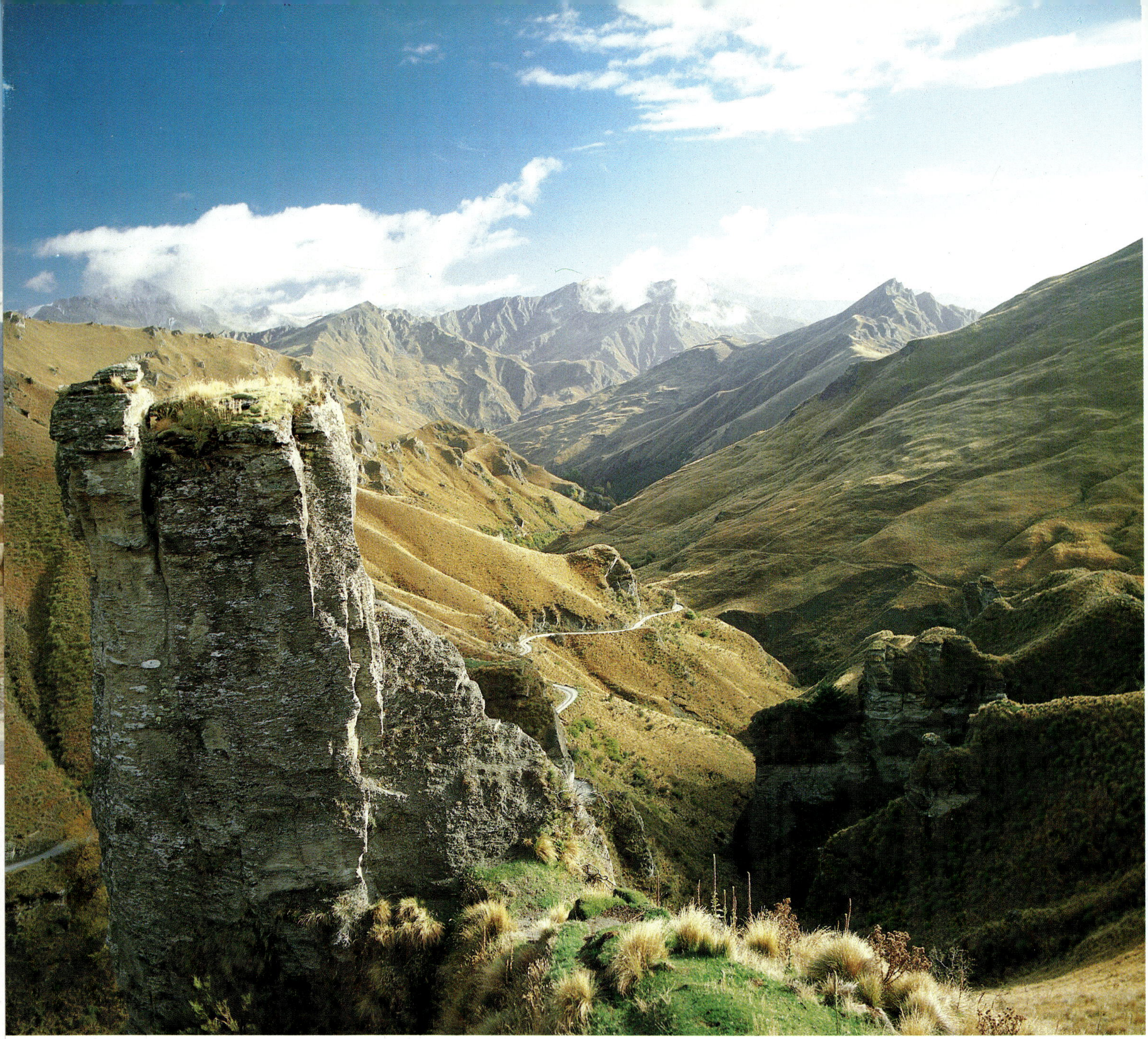

ABOVE: THE LIGHTHOUSE, SKIPPERS ROAD, QUEENSTOWN

The famous – or infamous – road that wanders and climbs precariously through Skippers Canyon leads into a harsh landscape, where the rocky frame of the mountains bursts out through the thin, parched soil, and rock formations have inspired fanciful names, like the Lighthouse. Perhaps the gold-fossickers found it comforting, in this unforgiving land, to imagine that such features might have been raised by men's hands rather than rudely sculpted, as they were, by climatic severity.

ABOVE RIGHT: REMARKABLES LANDSCAPE, NEAR QUEENSTOWN

As if relenting briefly, Central Otago now and again produces scenes of pastoral peace, such as these green and pleasant fields at the foot of the stern Remarkables Range – pockets of sun-trapped fertility amid the rugged mountains. The Remarkables, with peaks over 2000m (6560ft) high, and harsh, seamed faces, loom over Lake Wakatipu and make the soft pastures seem even more gentle by comparison. But even in these grassy fields, the hardy Merino and Corriedale do best, thriving where other breeds would succumb to the fierce alpine climate.

BELOW RIGHT: LAKE ALEXANDRINA, MACKENZIE COUNTRY

Lake Alexandrina, close to Lake Tekapo, forms a soft and comfortable oasis in the quilted landscape of brown hills. Even the water looks different from that of its neighbour, for this lake is rain-fed, not snow-fed. From the air, the contrasting colours of the snow-fed and rain-fed lakes of the Mackenzie Basin give an impression of jewels in a golden setting.

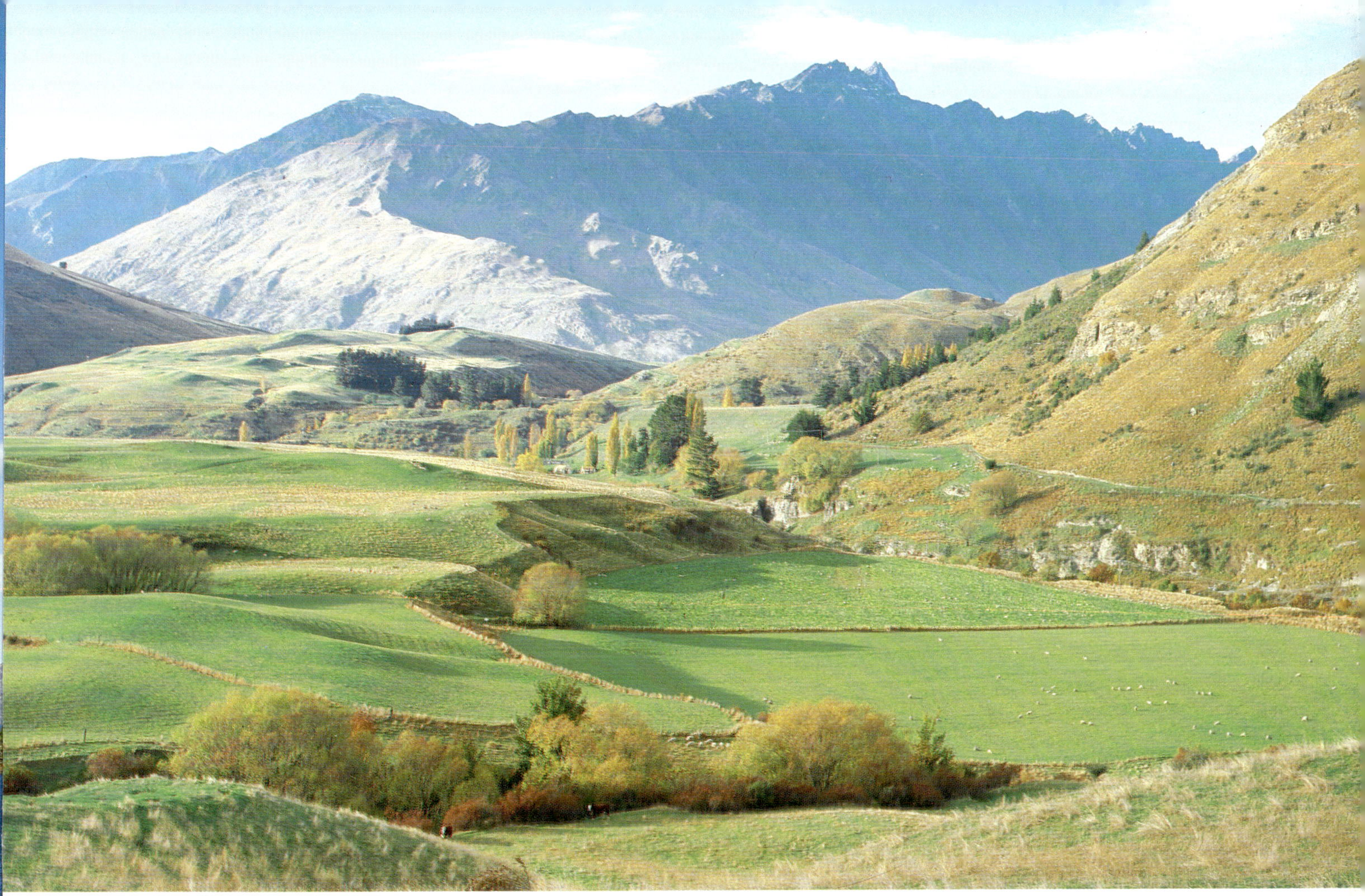

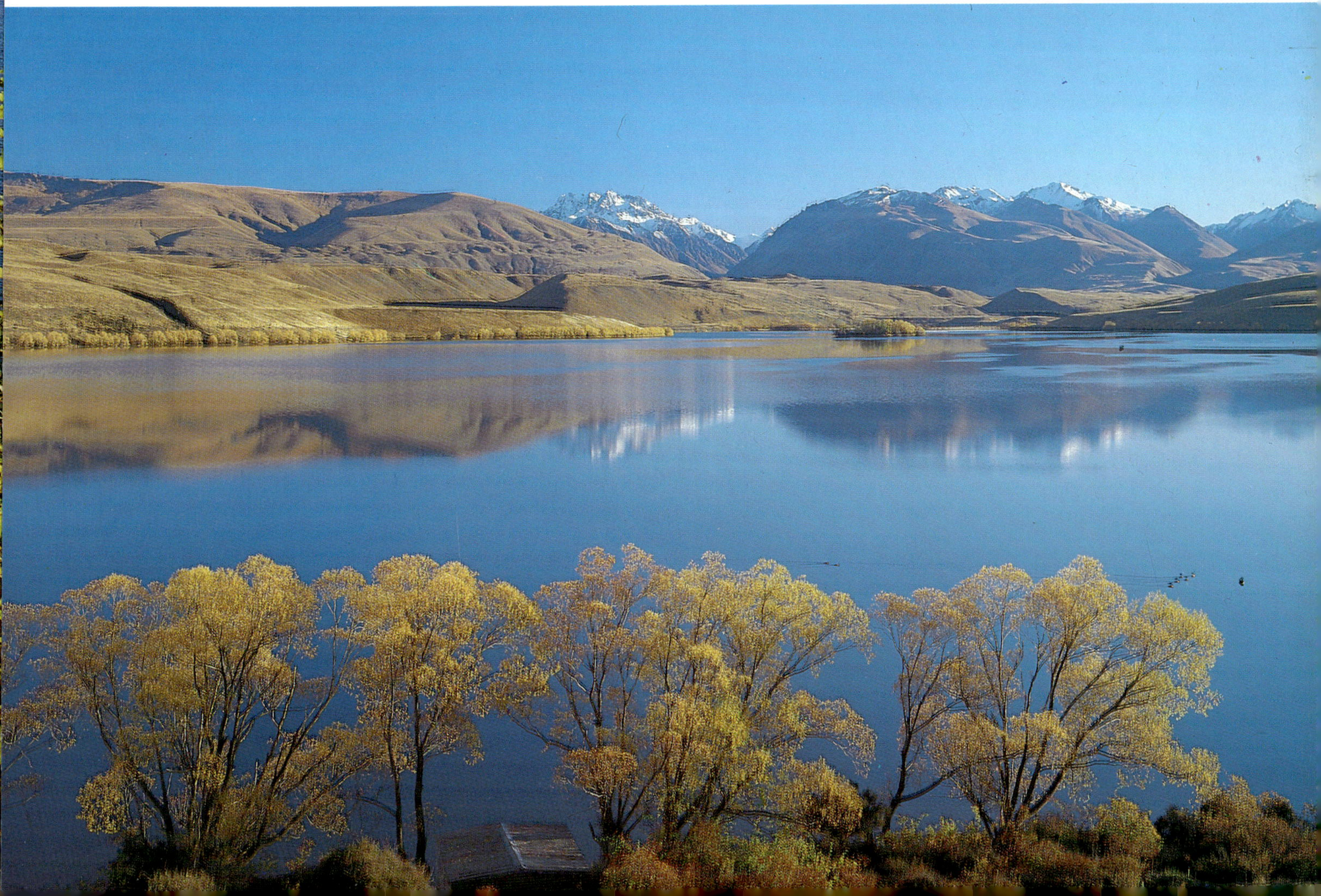

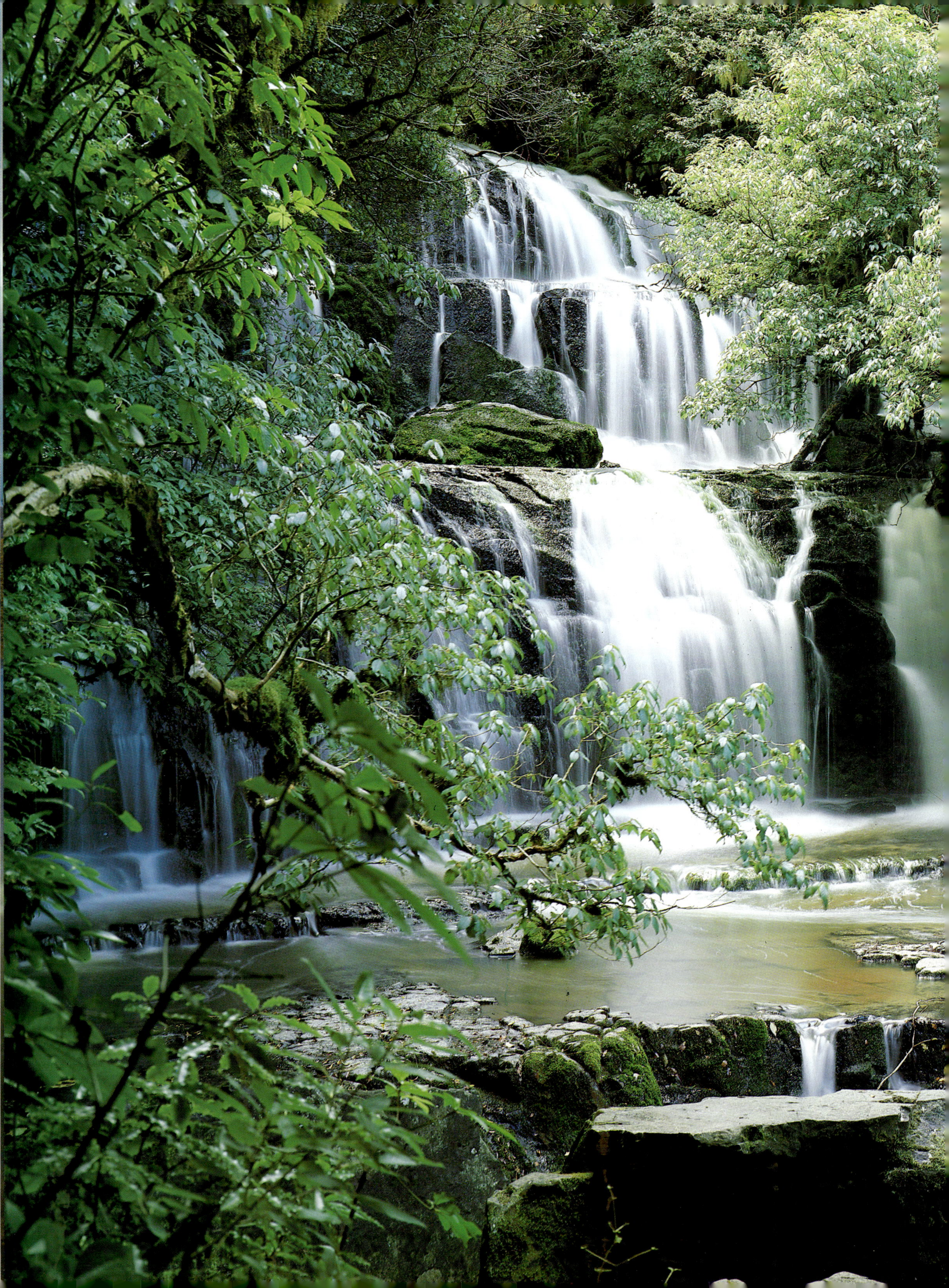

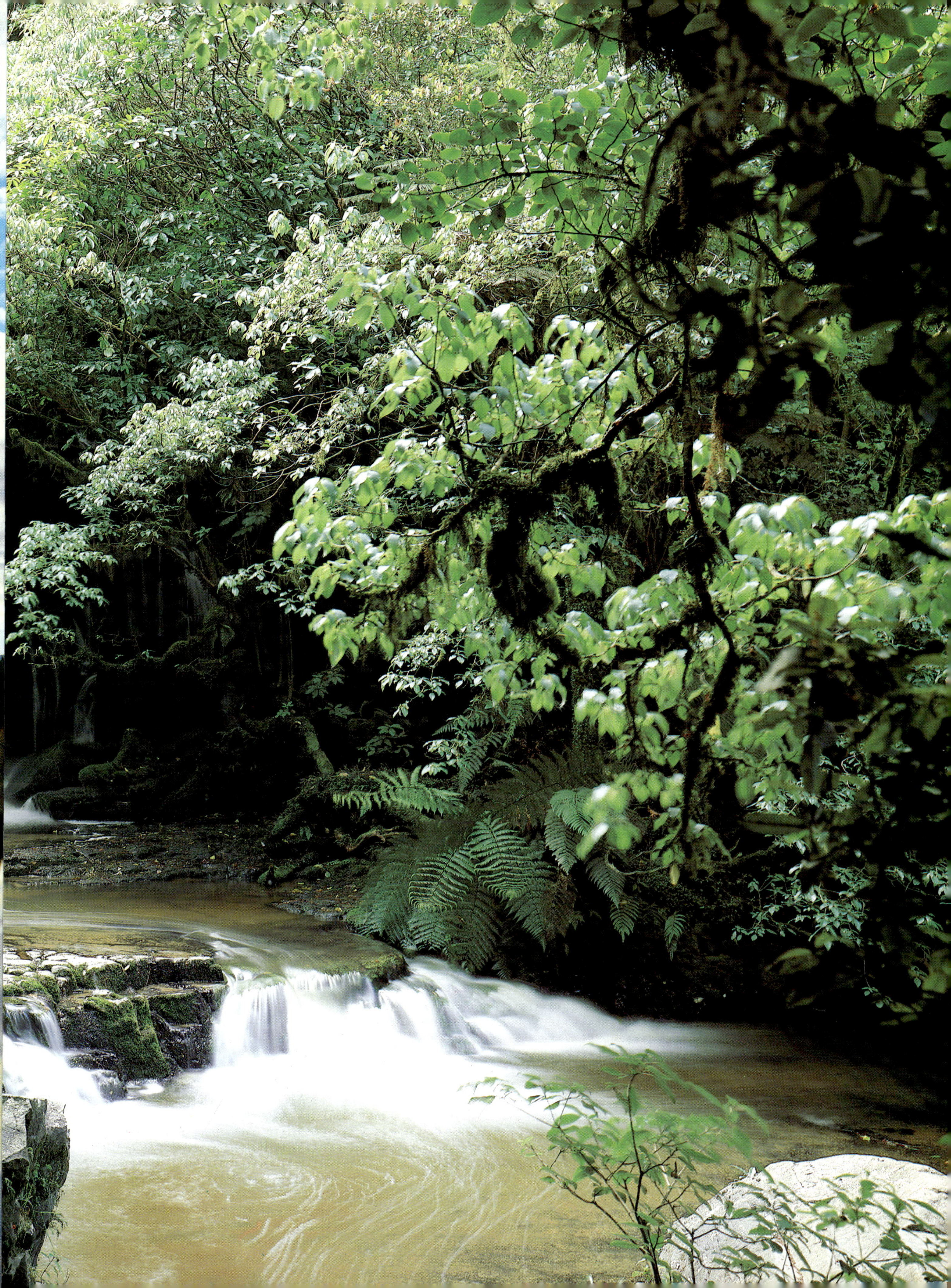

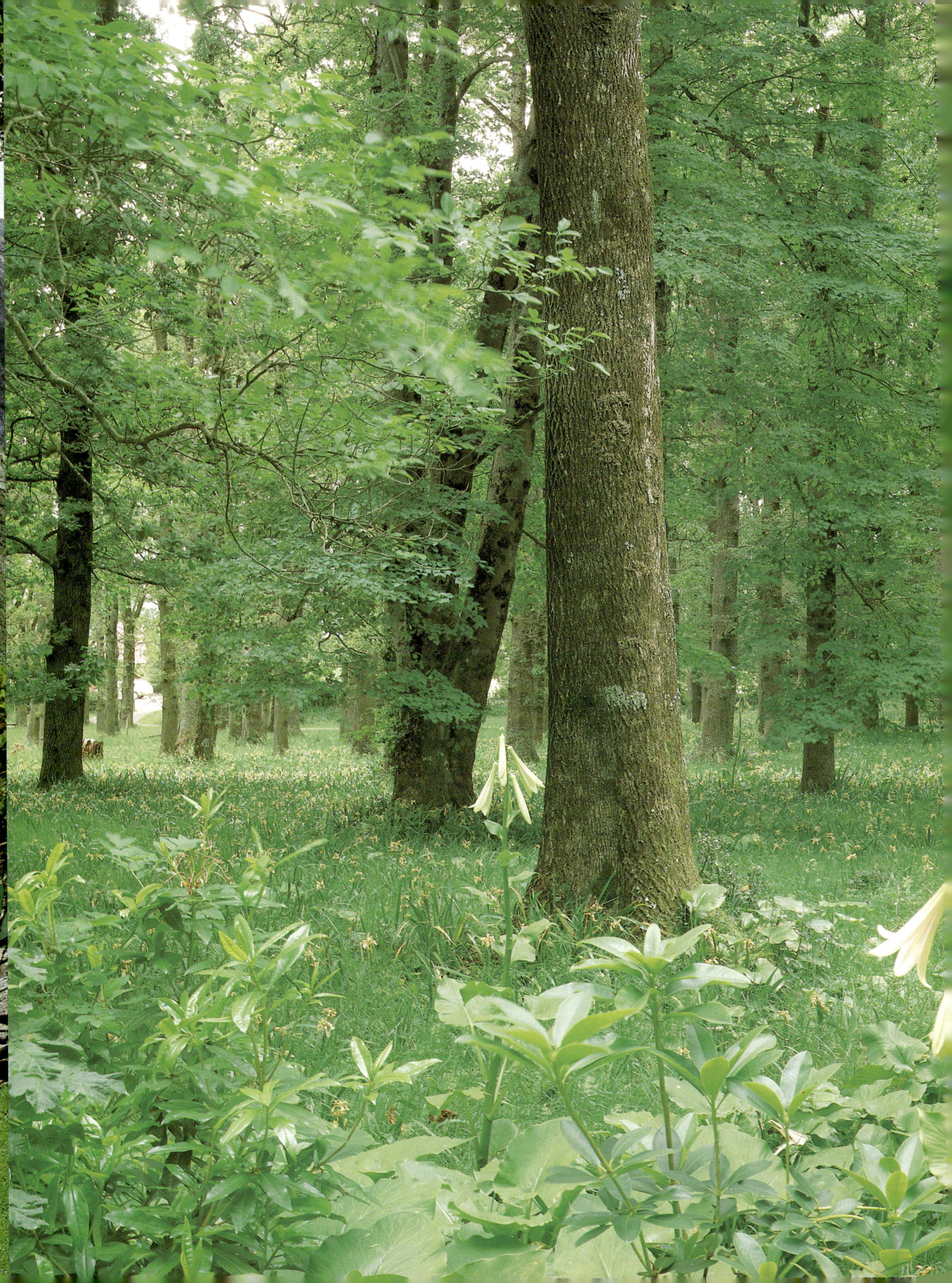

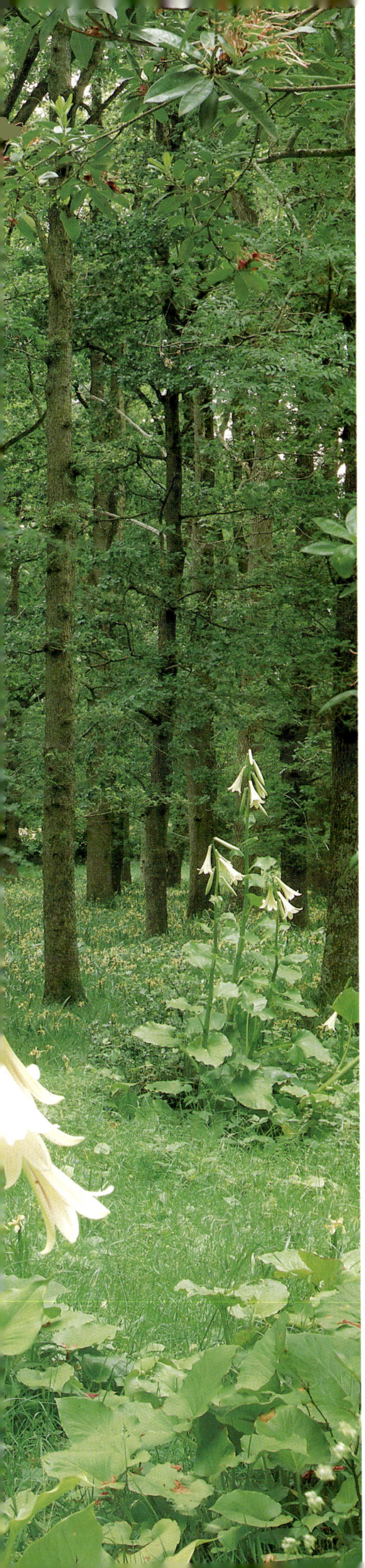

Order Amongst Natural Beauty

EVEN surrounded by a superabundance of natural beauty, people still have other needs. Man might not live by bread alone, but bread he must have to live at all. So the landscape is drilled and marshalled until it functions like machinery, to feed and clothe and house humankind. Also, though there are a few exceptional people for whom the untamed wilderness is all they need, there are many more for whom wild beauty is better taken in small sips. Most people, though they enjoy the grandeur of mountains and the riotous growth of the bush, have a need for ordered paths, tidy lawns and disciplined, flowery gardens.

In addition, those brave souls who first abandoned their familiar scenery to settle in a new and alien land experienced a crushing homesickness. To alleviate its very real pain, they hastened to establish in their new situation the style of buildings, the trees, flowers, animals and birds they had known and loved in the Old Country.

Yet it could never be a real duplication. For one thing, there was so much more land to spare. Farms were measured in thousands of acres, sheep runs in hundreds of square miles, rather than the neat, small, intensely cultivated holdings of rural England, measured in fifties or hundreds of acres. Every householder was encouraged to build his home on a half-acre or quarter-acre section, with the result that populations which would have fitted easily into a small cluster of semi-detached cottages bordering a quarter of a mile of English road, here sprawled over a square mile of perfectly farmable landscape; and the larger centres sprawled outward over areas that would have contained an English city.

Even architecture could not entirely reproduce the familiar English scene. The traditional methods of building were not entirely suitable. Nogging, for example, that style of building which is usually labelled 'Tudor', though it is much older than that, consisting of an exposed framing with the bricks laid in between the frame members, proved unsatisfactory in New Zealand because of the ferocious shrinkage of New Zealand timbers. The stone houses and ecclesiastical buildings which, in England, stood for centuries, could not cope with the earthquakes of this geologically younger land. So architecture and building practices became a sort of compromise, out of which grew some original and striking innovations.

LILY GIGANTUM, MT PEEL HOMESTEAD GROUNDS, CANTERBURY

Old World trees and Old World wildflowers create an English woodland in country which must have seemed, to the first Mt Peel settlers, to be a dreary, alien, tussock-covered wilderness at the feet of the overbearing mountains.

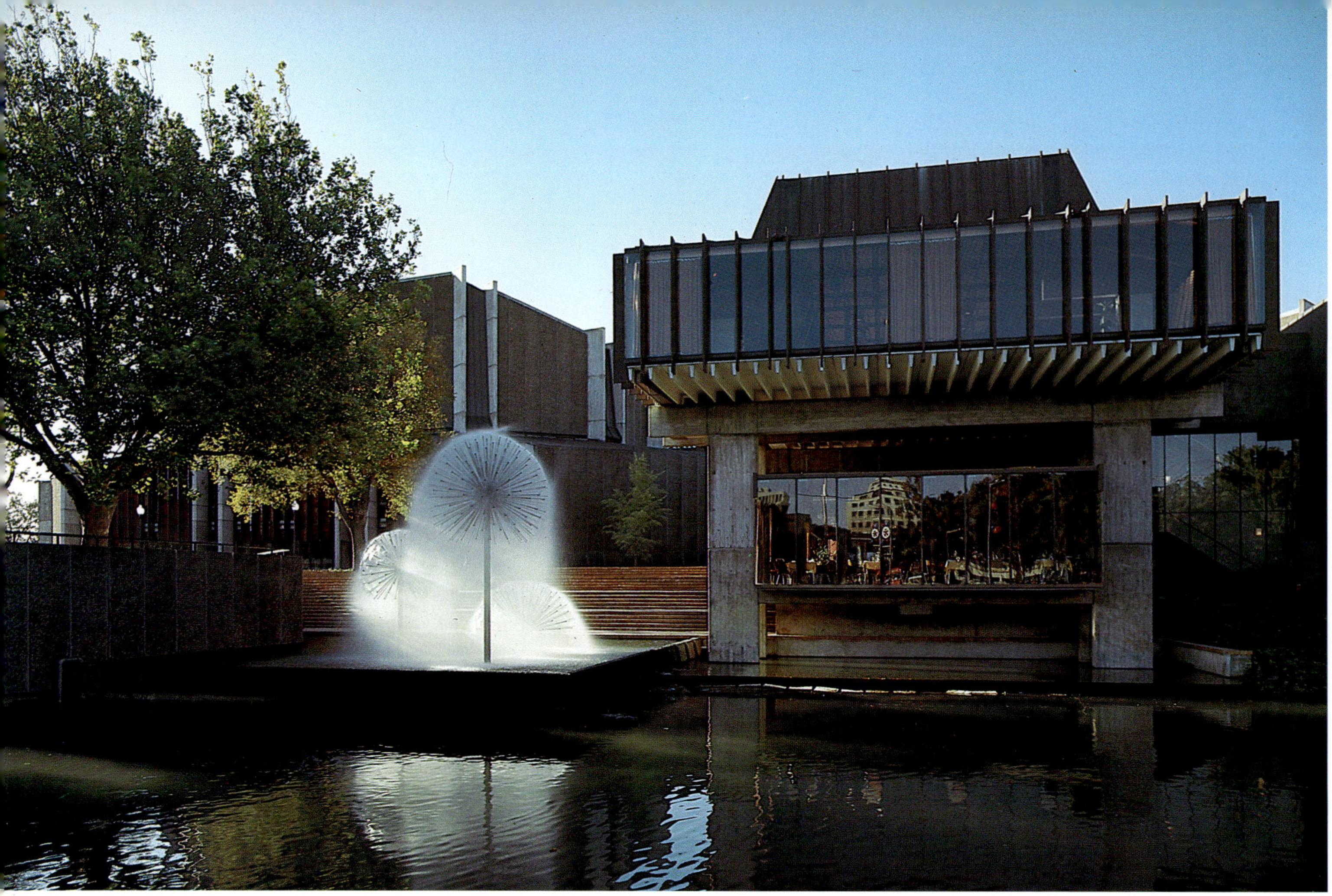

ABOVE: THE CHRISTCHURCH TOWN HALL AND FERRIER FOUNTAIN

On the banks of the principal stream, the settlers' descendants built their Town Hall complex, purely New Zealand in its architecture, yet somehow as English as a medieval castle. And in its courtyard, to offset its severity, they set fountains like giant thistledown.

RIGHT: DAFFODILS, BOTANICAL GARDENS, CHRISTCHURCH

On a swampy site, in heavy soil laced with a network of peaty streams, the Canterbury pioneers built a city. In its midst, they reserved 200 hectares (497 acres) of hard-won ground, to serve as a park and a garden, so that city dwellers would never lack for outdoor spaces; and in the middle of the park, they planted a garden of English trees, and patched the greensward with beds of daffodils so that spring in the heart of Christchurch would always remind them of April in England ...

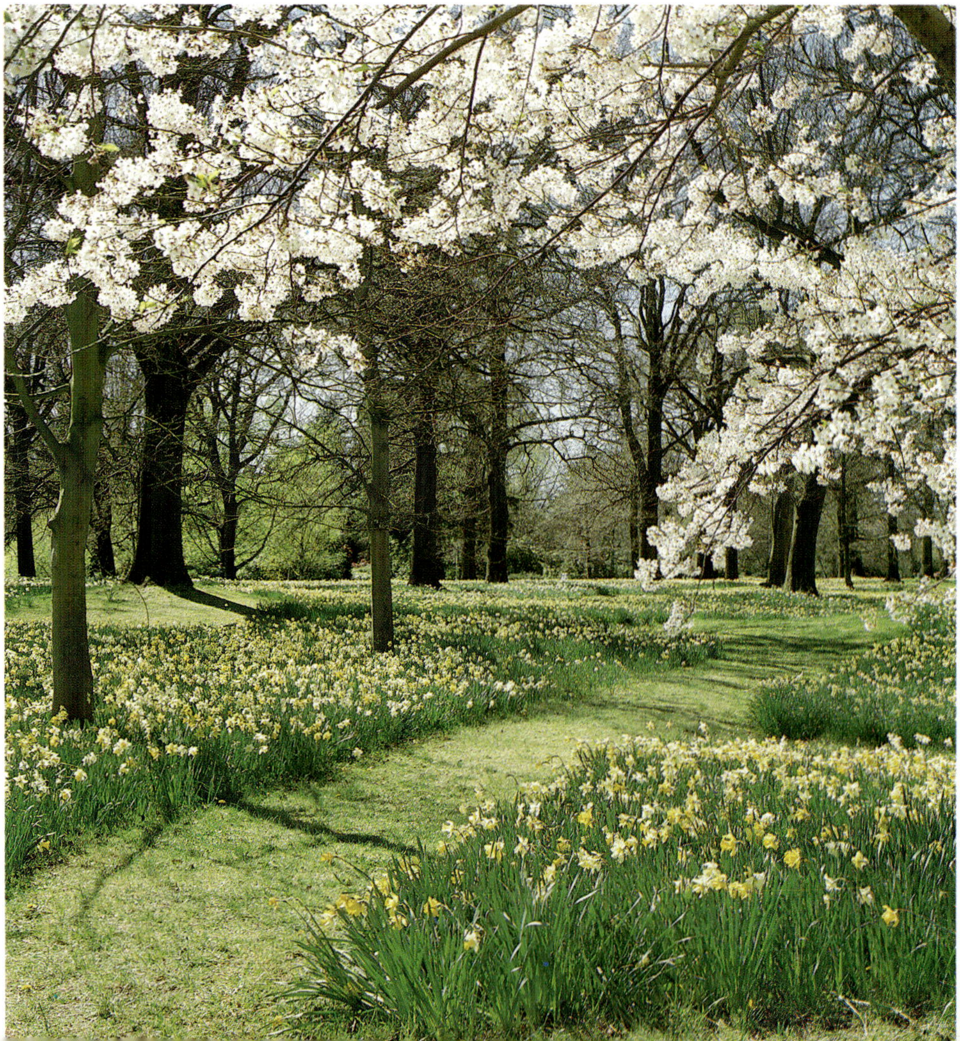

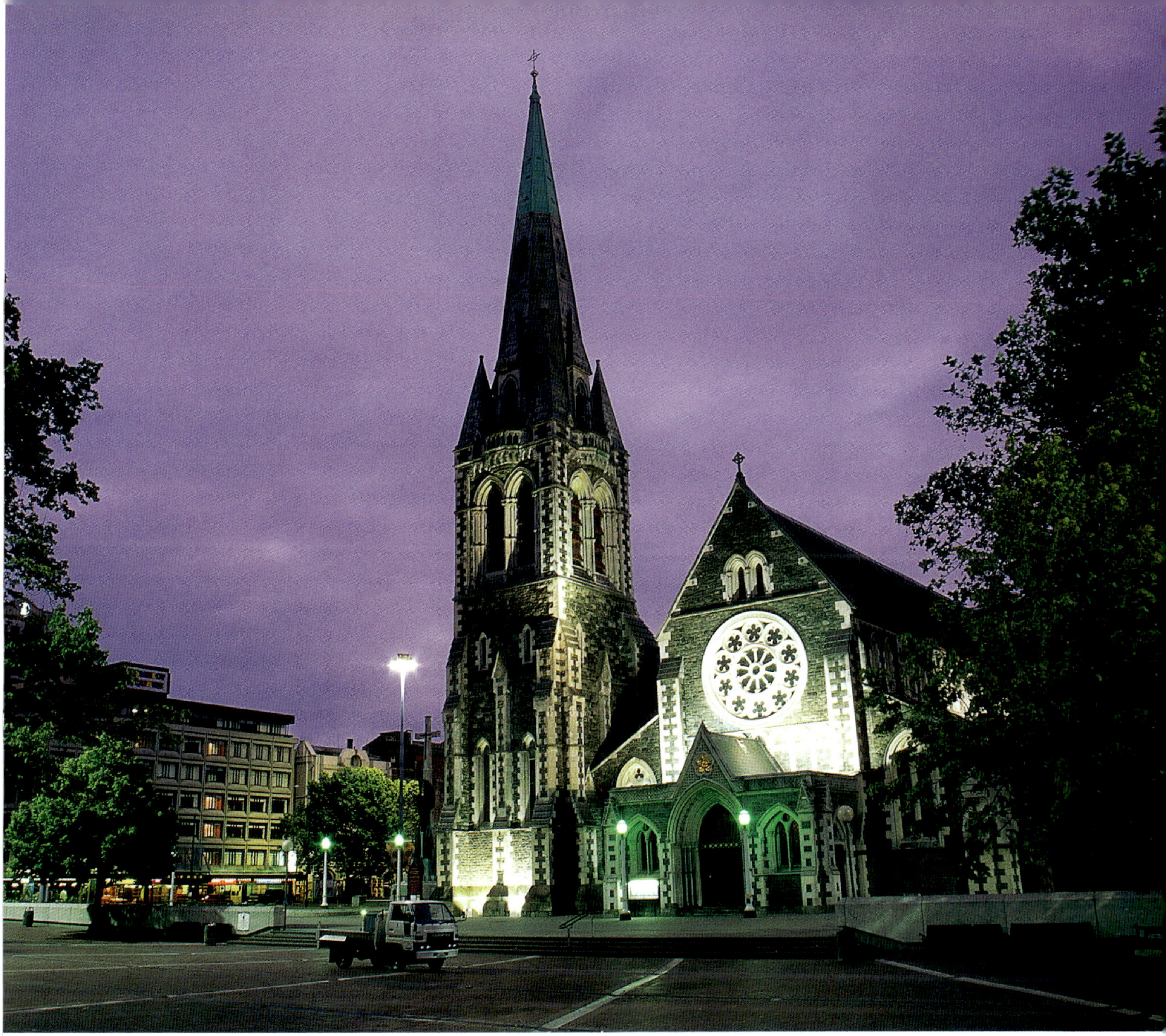

ABOVE: CHRISTCHURCH CATHEDRAL AND CATHEDRAL SQUARE

At the city's heart, they raised a Gothic cathedral, to denote the nature of their settlement and the direction of their own ideals. For the Canterbury pioneers were principally a Church of England band, and the Church originally undertook their pastoral and educational care. It was planned from the first that Christchurch should have a public school (English style) and a university; and the university chapel was to double as a cathedral. Circumstances changed these schemes somewhat, but the Christchurch Cathedral was built where the school and university were to have stood – in the centre of the city.

Some native trees did provide exceptionally fine building timbers; but the best of such timbers were slow-growing; and, moreover, early exploitation brought at least one species to the verge of extinction. Certain exotic trees, notably the radiata pine, were found to grow rapidly and well – so now vast areas have been planted in geometrically rectangular stands, tidily separated into dark green regiments by access roads and fire-breaks.

The rivers which flow mightily down to the ocean from upland lake and permanent snowfield have proved to be eminently harnessable for the production of electric power, or the irrigation of otherwise waste areas, or both. This has resulted in the creation of vast lakes, with resultant changes in weather patterns over certain areas.

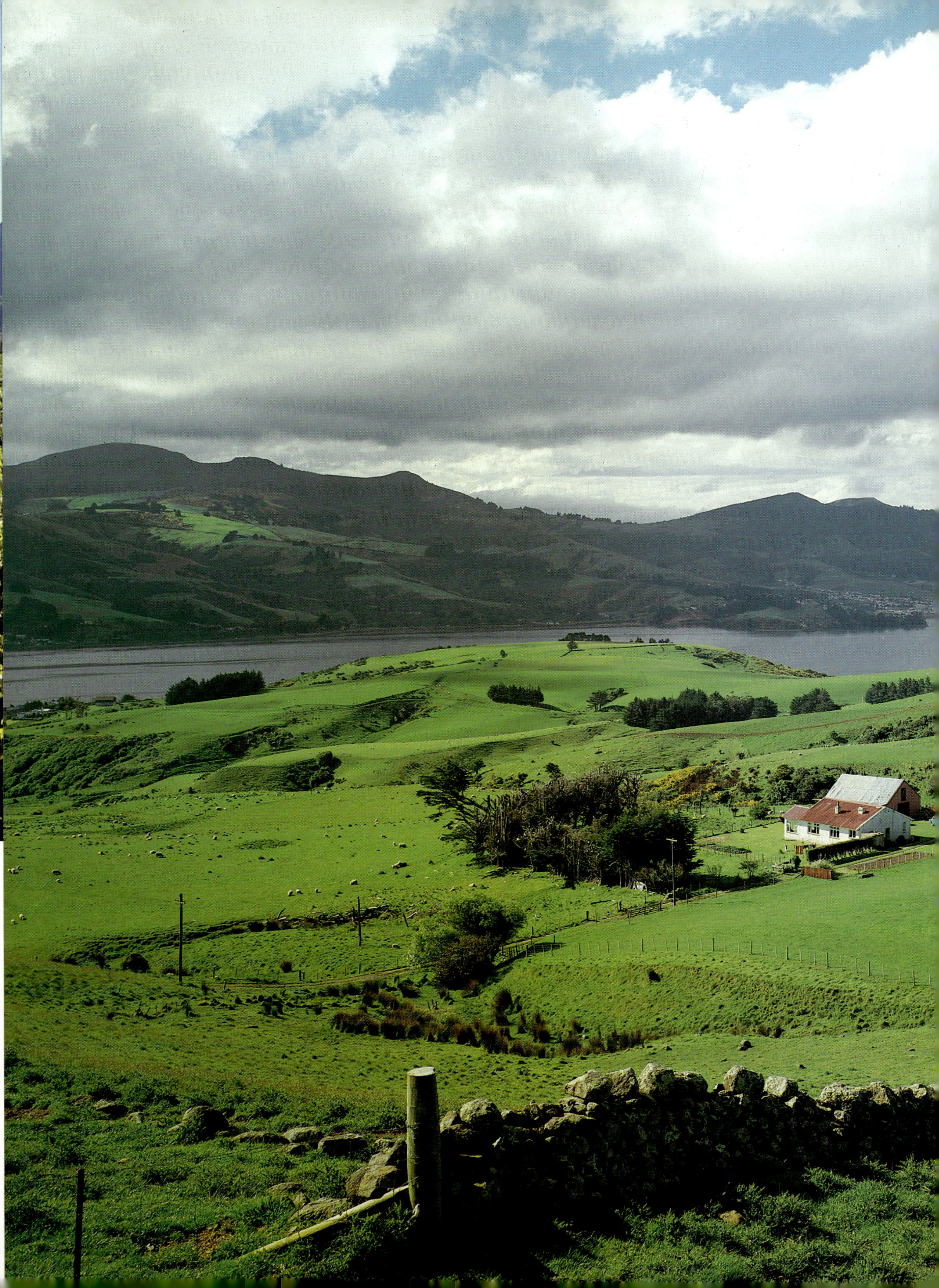

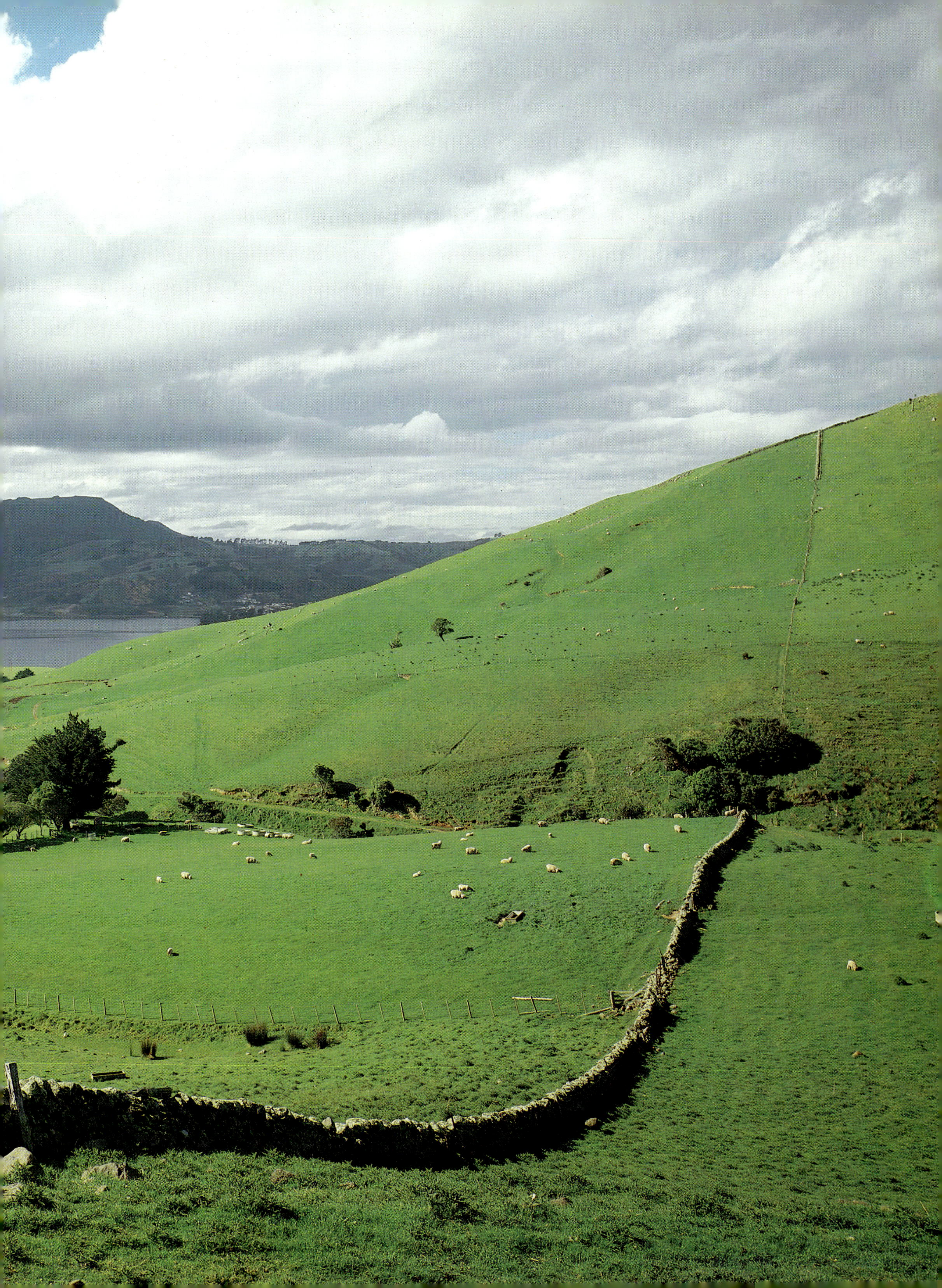

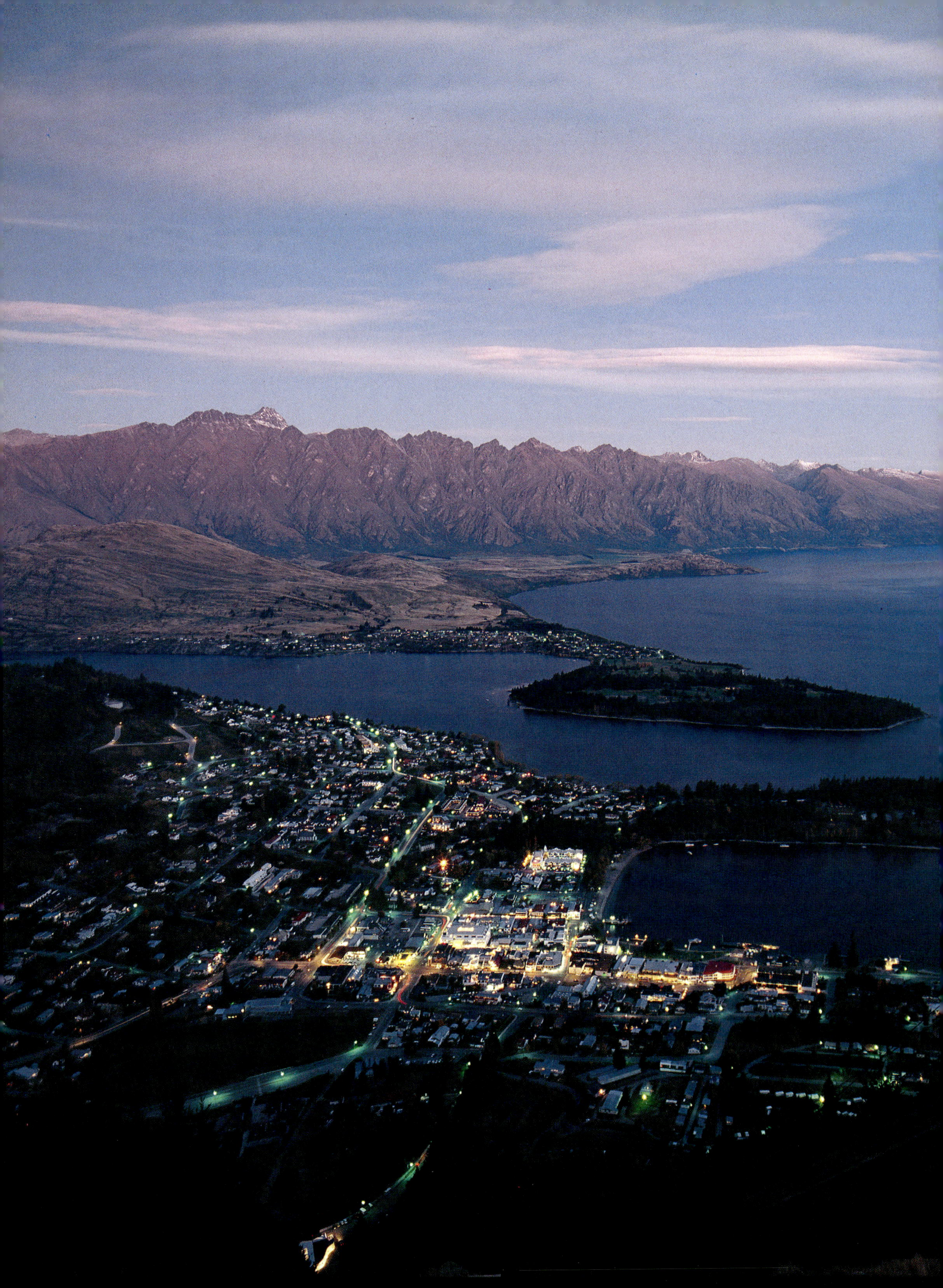

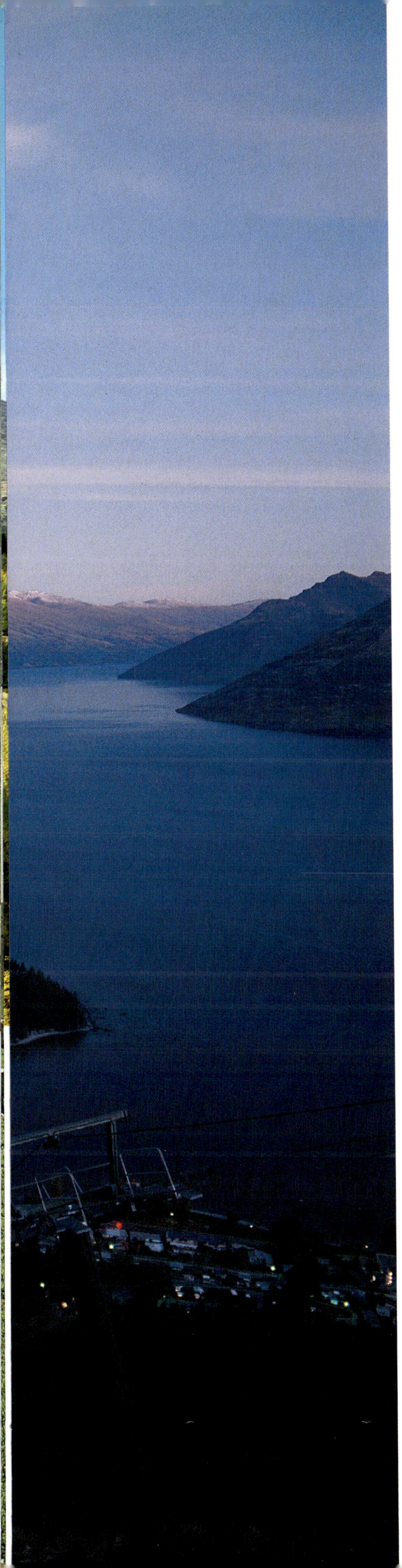

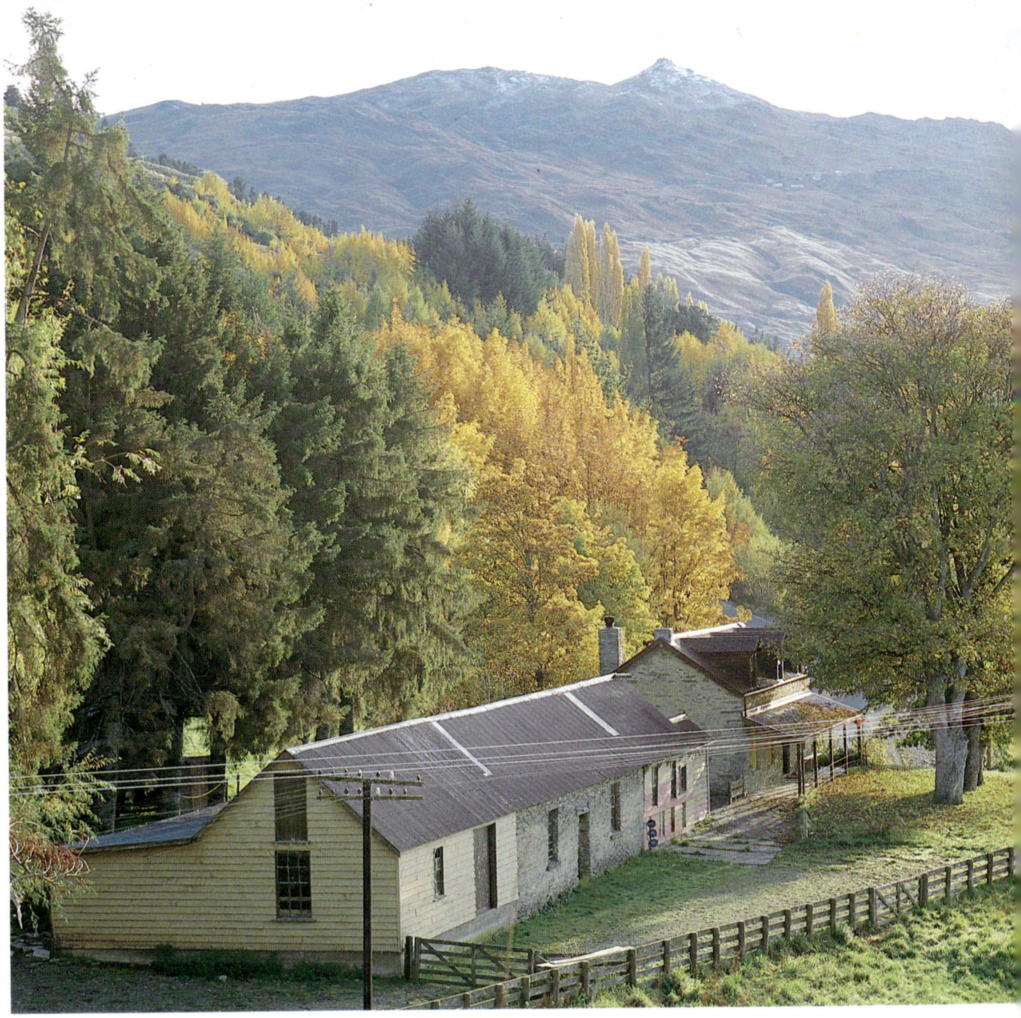

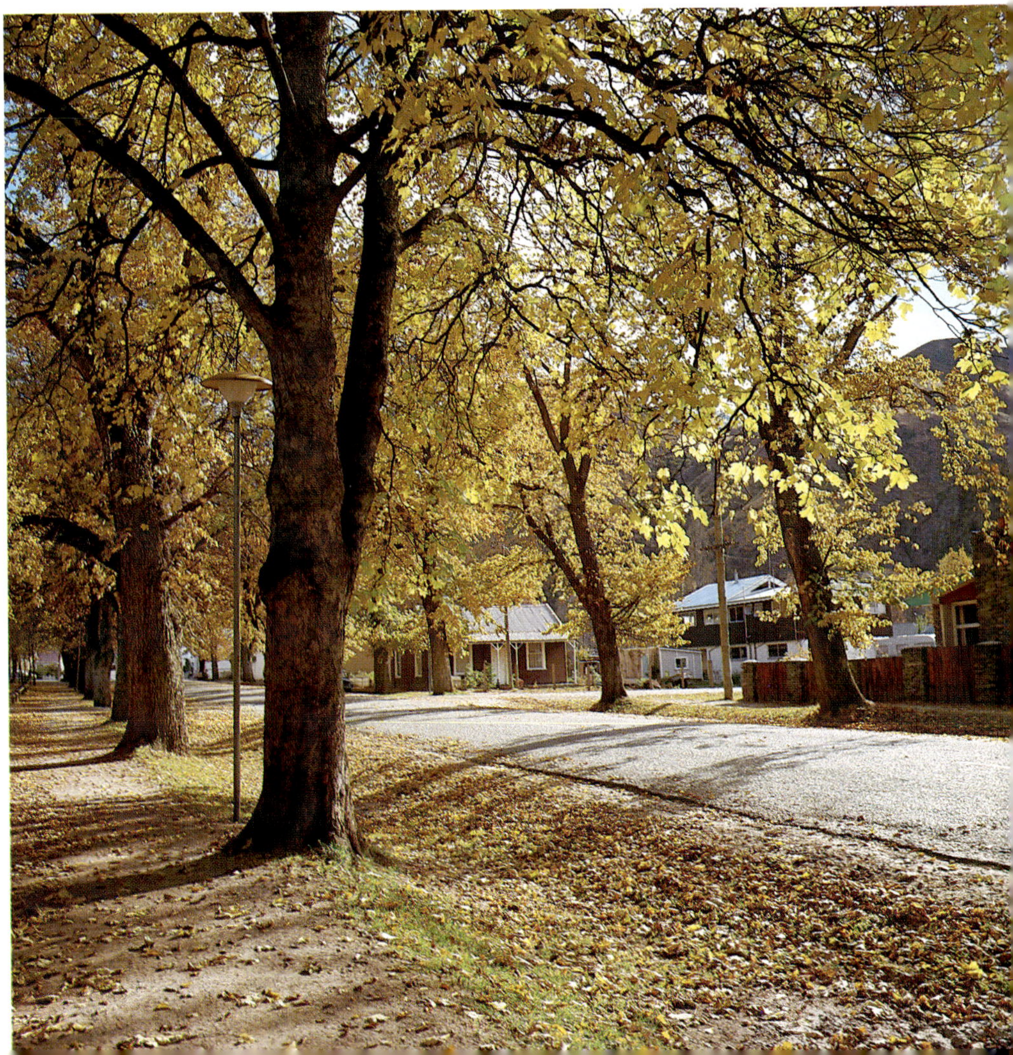

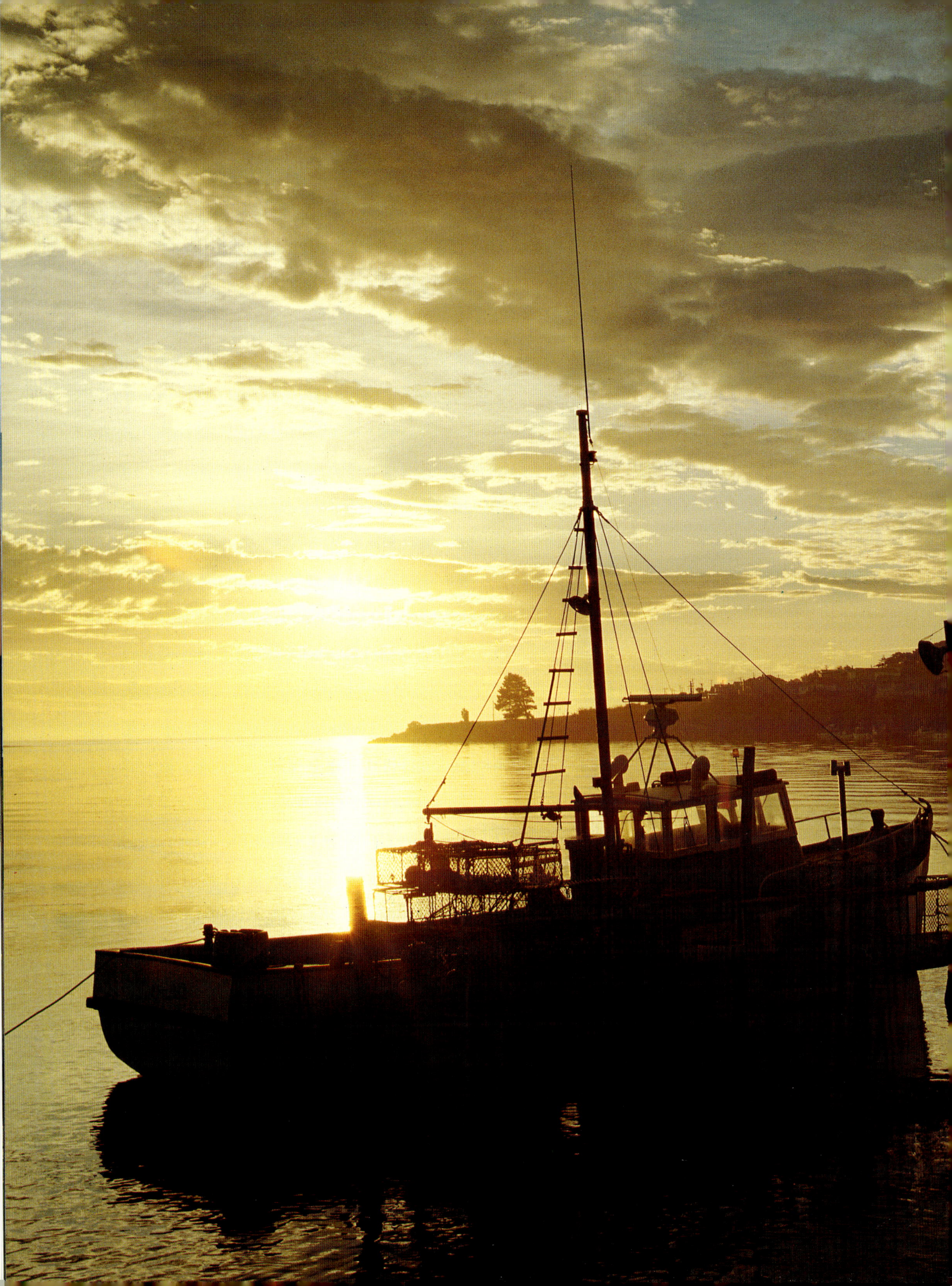

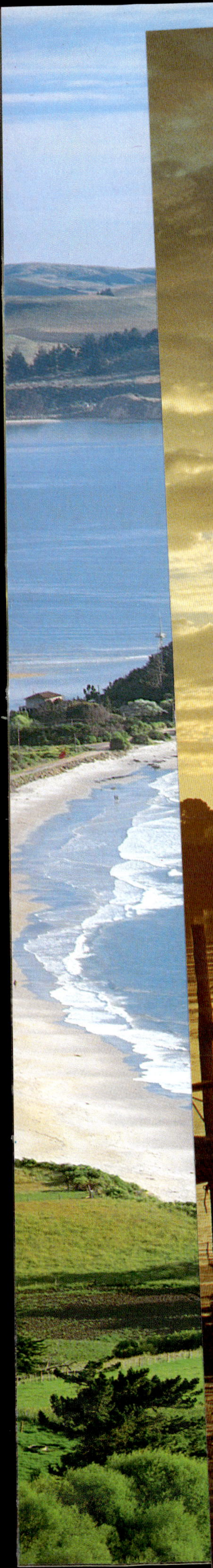

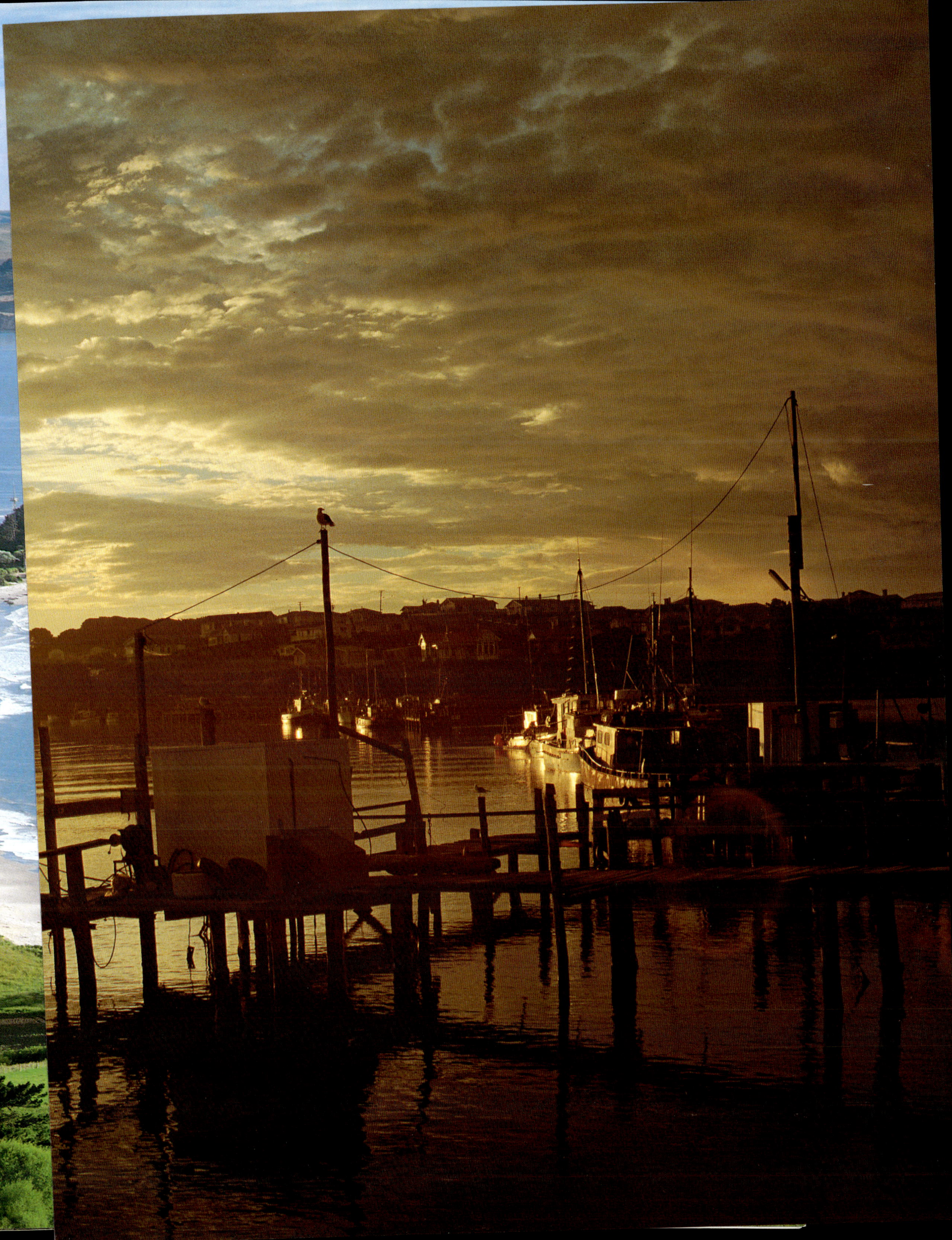

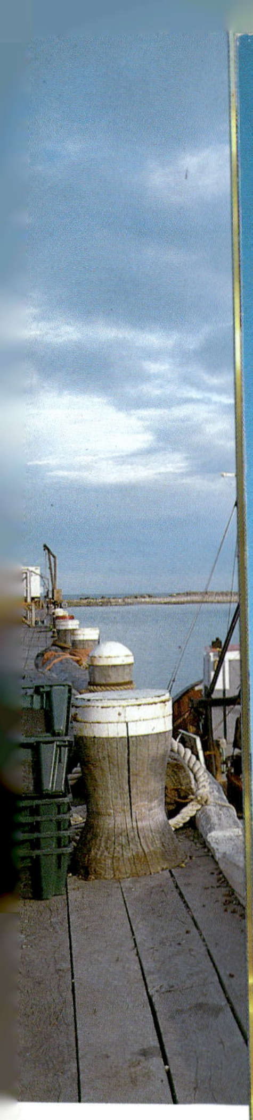

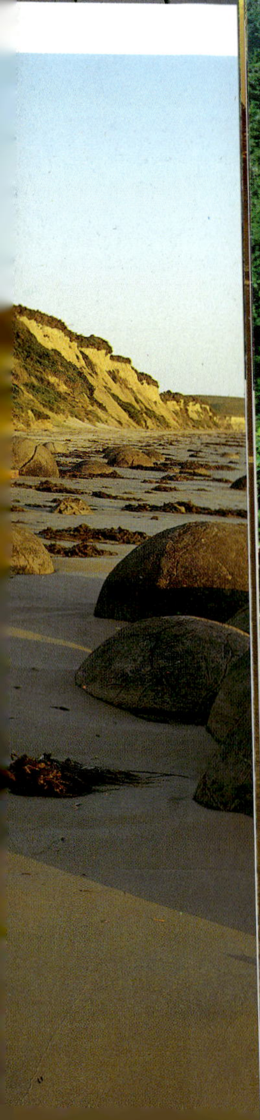

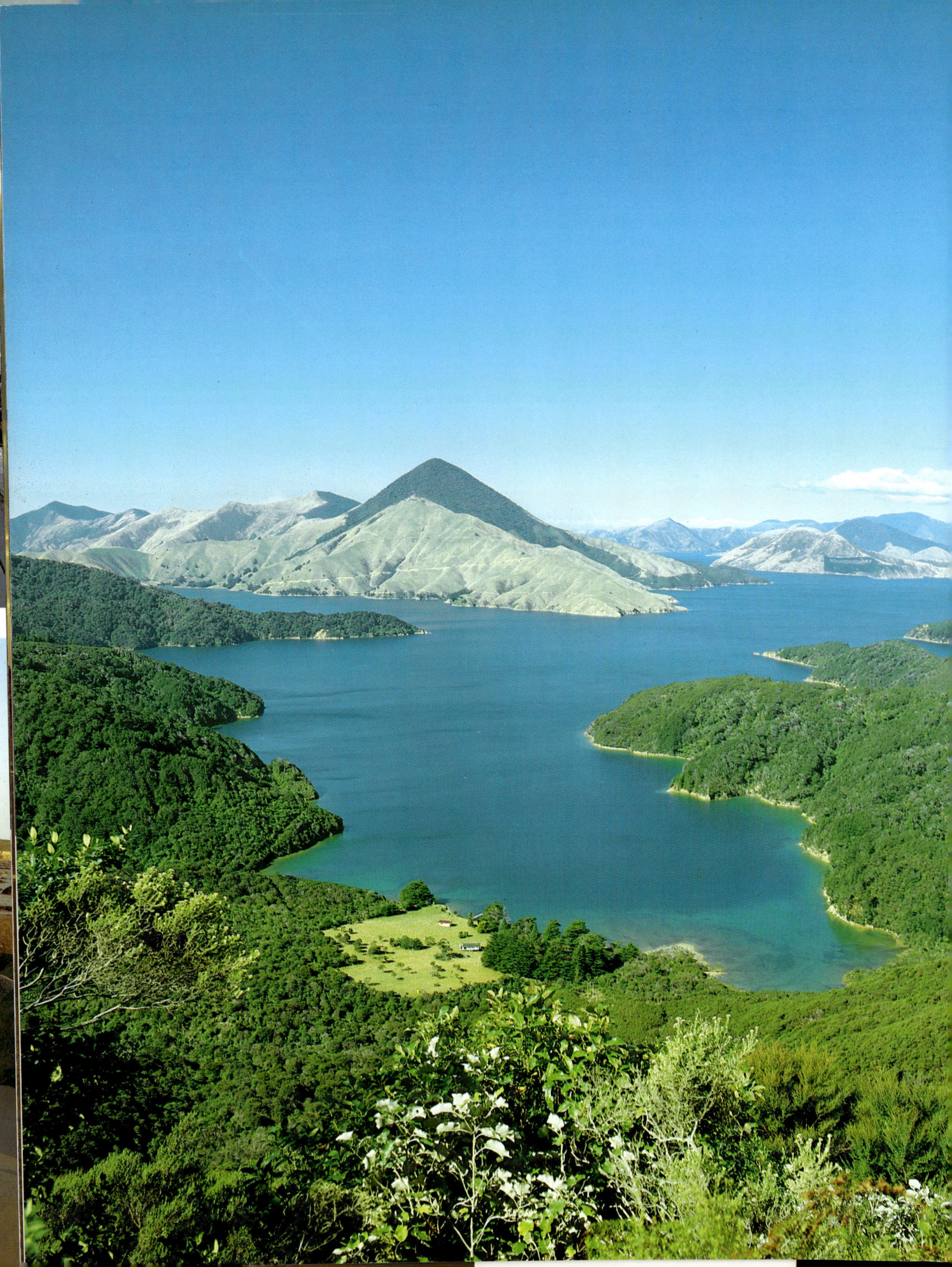

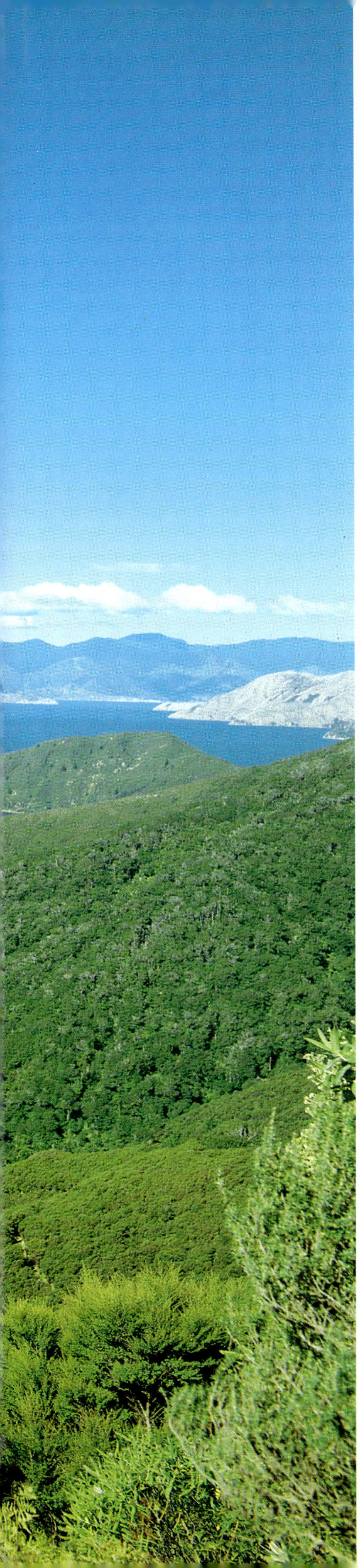

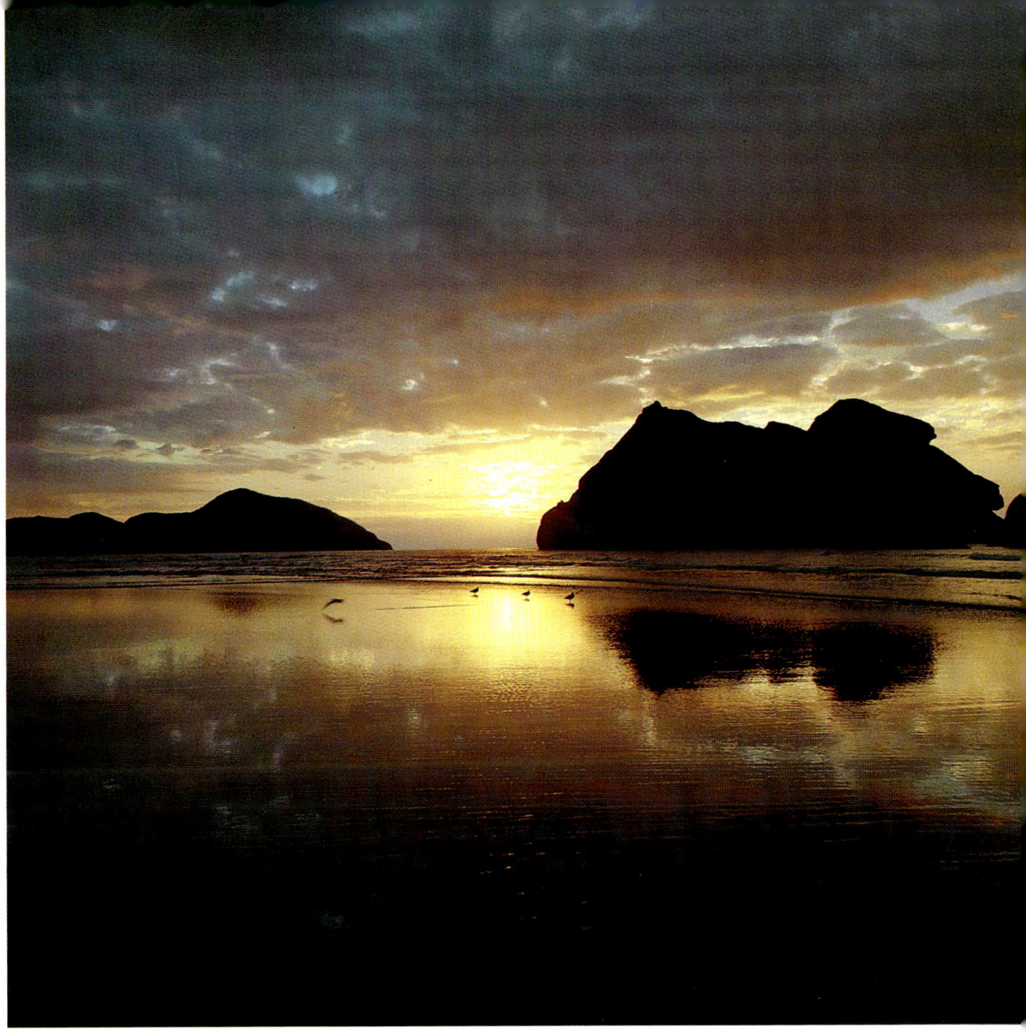

LEFT: MT SHEWELL AND FITZROY BAY, MARLBOROUGH SOUNDS

Fitzroy Bay is a complex harbour with many coves and inlets. A long spur from Mt Shewell, 775m (2542ft), runs down to Sheep Point, northern head of the almost land-locked bay. The hills, and the mountain itself, like most Marlborough Sounds countryside, are sun-browned pastures grazed by sheep, and patched with exotic and native forest.

ABOVE: WHARAIKI BEACH, CAPE FAREWELL

Wharaiki Beach, on the western side of Cape Farewell, looks out, past the offshore rocks, across the stormy Tasman Sea. The region is known for its beautiful sunsets. Cape Farewell was the last land sighted by Captain James Cook as he departed from New Zealand after his first exploratory voyage around the coast, and set sail for Australia.

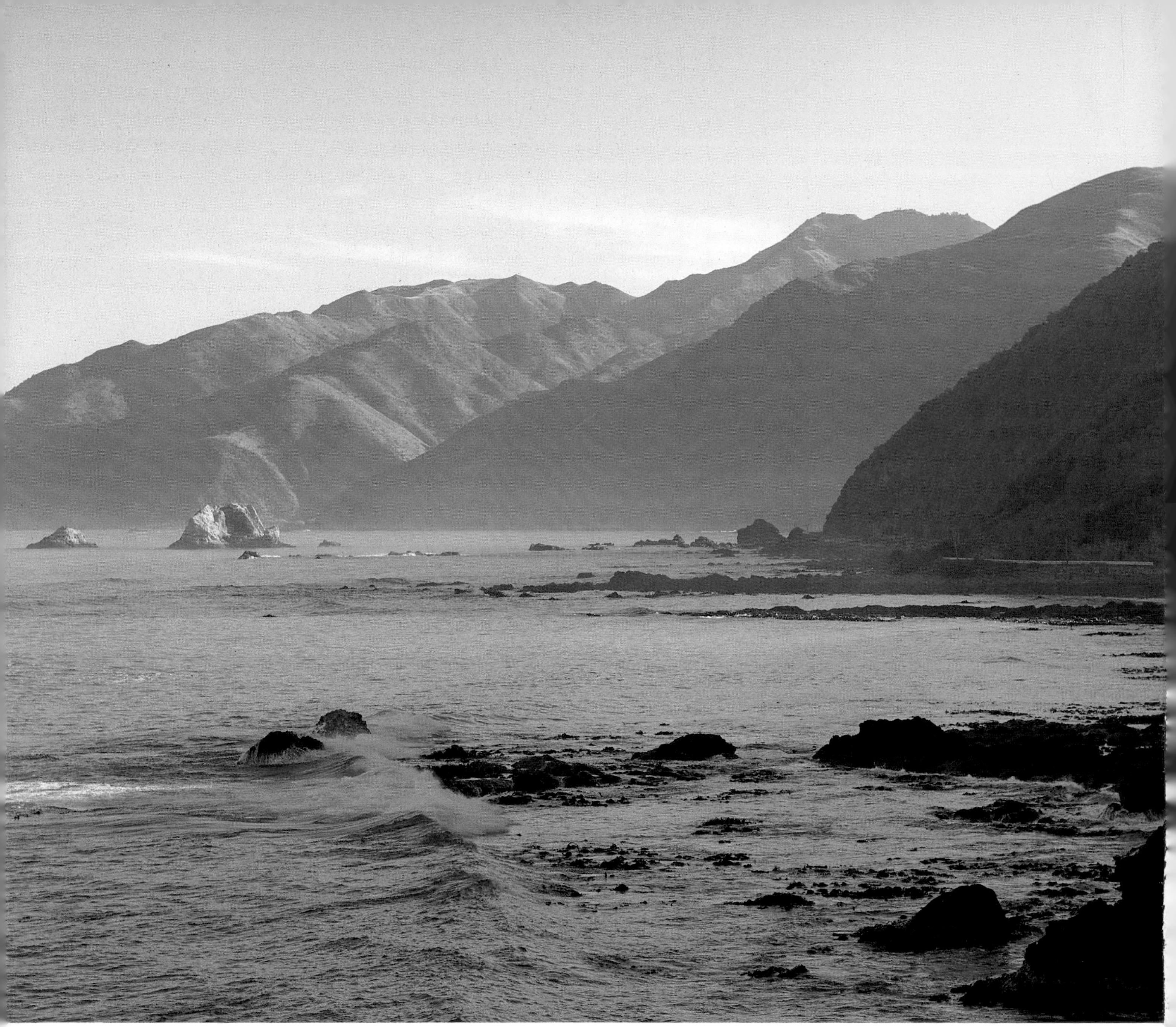

ABOVE: KAIKOURA COAST

The Inland and the Seaward Kaikoura Ranges run straight, parallel courses then drop down abruptly to the sea, south of where the Clarence River pours out from its high valleys. The coast here is a rugged rock-bound shore of jagged reefs and swirling kelp. Like England's Cornish coast, or the stormy coast of Maine, it is a place of deep little inlets where the crayfish, from which it gets its name (Kaikoura means 'feast of crayfish'), are still abundant.

This edition published in 2002 by New Holland Publishers (NZ) Ltd
Auckland • Sydney • London • Cape Town

218 Lake Road, Northcote, Auckland, New Zealand
14 Aquatic Drive, Frenchs Forest, NSW 2086, Australia
86–88 Edgware Road, W2 2EA, United Kingdom
80 McKenzie Street, Cape Town 8001, South Africa

First published in 1982 by Kowhai Publishing Ltd, reprinted 1985, 1987, 1992

ISBN 1 86966 011 0

Text design: Barbara Nielsen

Printed through Colorcraft, Hong Kong

10 9 8 7 6 5 4 3 2 1